French politics today

Wide-ranging, up-to-date and accessible, ~~~~ ~~~~ offers the student
an attractive introduction to the French political scene. Peter Morris
provides a clear description and readable analysis of the institutions
and processes, and draws attention to issues and controversies on the
current policy agenda.

Topics covered in the book include the evolution of French political
traditions; the constitutional settlement of the Fifth Republic; the
emergence of the modern presidency and its relationship to other
government institutions; the shape of local government; the shifting
contours of the party system; the emergence of Jean Marie le Pen's
Front National; and France and the European Community. Throughout the book, the author highlights the events and trends which have
shaped the French political system.

Politics today

Series editor: Bill Jones

French politics today

Peter Morris

Manchester University Press
Manchester and New York

Distributed exclusively in the USA and Canada by St. Martin's Press

Published by Manchester University Press
Oxford Road, Manchester M13 9NR, UK
and Room 400, 175 Fifth Avenue, New York, NY 10010, USA

Distributed exclusively in the USA and Canada
by St. Martin's Press, Inc., 175 Fifth Avenue, New York,
NY 10010, USA

British Library Cataloguing-in-Publication Data
A catalogue record for this book is available from the British Library

Library of Congress Cataloging-in-Publication Data

Morris, Peter, 1946–
    French politics today / Peter Morris.
        p.   cm. — (Politics today)
    ISBN 0–7190–3763–8 (hb.). — ISBN 0–7190–3764–6 (pbk.)
    1. France — Politics and government — 1981– I. Title. II. Series:
    Politics today (Manchester, England)
    JN2594.2. M65 1993.
    320. 444 — dc20   93–40663

ISBN 0 7190 3763 8 *hardback*
    0 7190 3764 6 *paperback*

Typeset in Great Britain
by The Midland Book Typesetting Company

Printed in Great Britain
by Bell & Bain Ltd, Glasgow

Contents

Preface and acknowledgements

This book seeks to describe and explain the main elements of French politics. The processes it describes have always had the capacity to provoke controversy inside France and to mystify outsiders nurtured on the apparent certainties of Anglo-American politics. Yet the very 'otherness' of French politics is what gives the subject its abiding fascination. It helps us to understand how, and why, a democratic political system can work differently from what the French often call, with a mixture of admiration and irritation, the 'Anglo-Saxon' countries.

French politics has always attracted the attention of distinguished scholars from Britain and the United States and the present text shows my great indebtedness to their work. I wish to thank my friends and colleagues Dennis Kavanagh, Robert Elgie, Raymond Kuhn and Peter Fysh for their helpful comments on individual chapters. I am also grateful to the editors at Manchester University Press for inviting me to write the book and to David Bell for going through the manuscript with a scrupulously learned eye. As always, I thank my wife Rosie for making everything better.

1

France: What kind of past?

France, like Britain but unlike Germany or Italy, is one of the oldest states in Europe. Its geographical and political identity was clearly established by the late Middle Ages, and its frontiers, with the exception of the eastern region of Alsace Lorraine, have not significantly changed since the early 1800s. The celebrated palace of Versailles, constructed near Paris by King Louis XIV (1643–1715), remains the symbol of France's political unity in the same way that the Palace of Westminster does in the United Kingdom. Despite losing in the nineteenth century the pre-eminence in international relations which it had earlier enjoyed, France remains, like Britain, a major European power with important extra-European strategic and economic interests, a permanent seat on the Security Council of the United Nations and a powerful role in the European Community.

In common with other European systems, France is a constitutional democracy. Universal suffrage and free competitive elections legitimise the exercise of public power; the Government is accountable to the popularly elected branch of a bicameral legislature; the courts are an independent part of the Executive. As elsewhere in western Europe, France has an extensive welfare state in which government is responsible for the organisation of social services that are paid for out of central taxation.

The economy is similar to that of its neighbours in that it is a market system based on private enterprise and is dominated by manufacturing and service industries. France is the world's fourth largest exporter of manufactured goods and its banks are amongst the largest in Europe. Despite the tenacious image of France as a rural country, and the importance of agriculture to its exports, only 6.85 per cent of the labour force works on the land: 82 per cent of the total population of over fifty-six million live in cities.

It is necessary to stress at the outset the similarities between France and its neighbours for the simple reason that its political institutions and arrangements can appear very different from those existing elsewhere, and notably in Britain. Perhaps the two most obvious differences separating France from Britain are (a) the former's long tradition of constitutional instability and (b) the important role played by the State in the organisation of French society. The first point is demonstrated by the fact that the present regime is known as the Fifth Republic and that its thirty-five years' existence make it the second longest lasting of the seventeen regimes that have governed France since the Revolution of 1789. The second point is shown by the centrality in France's political vocabulary of the idea of the State and by the continuing ability of central government to intervene across a variety of sectors that elsewhere are left to private individuals and organisations.

These differences, and there are many others, make France an interesting country to the student of politics. They also explain why it is difficult to be neutral about French politics. Admirers of France have pointed to its role in introducing democratic politics to the world and, more recently, to the ability of its State since 1945 to mobilise national resources in a successful programme of economic modernisation. The numerous critics of the French experience of politics have focussed instead on the instability and violence that have marked its political evolution and on the authoritarianism that has characterised the exercise of governmental power.

The purpose of this first chapter is to outline the traditions that have helped to shape the way in which contemporary French politics is organised and perceived. The present is not, of course, simply a re-run of the past and one of the constant themes of this book will be the importance of the changes that have occurred in the institutional and political arrangements in recent decades. France in 1993 is a very different polity – and society – from what it was in 1958–59 when the Fifth Republic came into being. A leading British expert on French politics has argued that we now see in France the 'exhaustion of the revolutionary heritage' that was so important in explaining its recent past (Hayward 1991, p. 15). But far-off events and conflicts can still influence current practice and there can be no doubt that the vocabulary of French politics is still influenced by its past – and by interpretations of that past. General de Gaulle reflected what many feel when he described France as being weighed down (*accablée*) by its history.

The legacy of the French Revolution

It is often said that, just as the United States of America dates from the Declaration of Independence in 1776, so modern French politics begins with the French Revolution of 1789. Such a claim ignores both the role of the French Monarchy in creating France's national and administrative identity and the fact that pre-revolutionary France was the dominant European power. Yet the Revolution is unquestionably an event of great importance in the creation of modern France (and Europe) even though historians have always disagreed over the extent to which it actually transformed the social – or administrative – structure of old France.

It is not enough, however, simply to state that the Revolution was important. We need to know in what ways it influenced France's constitutional and political evolution. Its broader impact on Europe's development cannot be discussed here; suffice it to say that its message of political liberation was intended to be universal, and not merely national, in scope and that, like the Bolshevik Revolution of October 1917, it posed a direct challenge to existing political orders throughout, and beyond, Europe.

Wordsworth's famous lines on the revolution 'bliss was it in that dawn to be alive/but to be young was very heaven' convey the excitement generated across Europe by the overthrow of the *ancien régime* and the end of the absolutist monarchy of the Bourbons. The fall of the royal fortress of the Bastille on 14 July 1789 (France's national day) remains a symbolic event of great significance. The French Revolution was carried out in the name of the Rights of Man and the Citizen: 1789 saw the rejection of the idea that the Monarchy was entitled to expect the obedience of the people on the grounds that the king was the agent of God's purpose. Government's legitimacy, its claim to authority, derived henceforth from the consent of the Nation. The *ancien régime* had been based on the division of society into legal categories, known as estates. Membership of the first and second estates (clergy and nobility) conferred legal and social entitlements that were not available to the Third Estate – in which nine-tenths of the population were to be found. In 1789, the privileges of the first two estates were abolished and a country of rulers, subjects and estates was replaced by a nation of citizens. 'Liberty, Equality, Fraternity' and 'The Rights of Man' became the principle, and the goal, of political activity.

What makes the legacy of the Revolution important for the study of French politics is, firstly, the fact that it caused great upheaval inside and outside France. The events of the early 1790s – the attack on the institutional privileges of the Roman Catholic Church, the overthrow of the Monarchy and the establishment of a Republic, the notorious Terror (with which the guillotine is identified) – suggested to many inside and outside France that the French Revolution had unleashed a lethal political virus. European Conservatism found its pamphleteer of genius in Edmund Burke whose *Reflections on the Revolution in France* (1791) argued that any attempt to restructure society by rejecting tradition in the name of the abstract principle of the rights of man must end in disaster. Burke's prescience, and subsequent reputation, derive from the fact that his book was written before the period of the Terror, the subsequent emergence of which seemed to vindicate the Conservatives' detestation of the Revolution. As recently as 1989 Mrs Thatcher, who in her youth had been strongly influenced by Charles Dickens' account of the Paris Terror in 'A Tale of Two Cities', denounced the damage done to Europe by the Revolution.

For a long time after the Revolution, France appeared to other European states to be a potentially menacing and destabilising threat to international stability. The universalist claims made at the time about the Revolution's goal of liberating Humanity and Nations from the oppression of their rulers seemed to its opponents a cloak for French expansionism. Napoleon's defeat at Waterloo in 1815 marked the definitive end to France's status as a superpower and for over a century now her foreign policy has been dominated by the threatening reality of her powerful neighbour Germany. Yet the myth of an aggressively nationalist France has persisted into the late twentieth-century. From General de Gaulle onwards, presidents of the Fifth Republic have emphasised their commitment to national 'grandeur' and to the independent role that France must play in the international system (see Chapter 10).

Within France itself, conservative groups insisted that the revolutionary values of citizen democracy and anti-Catholicism were the agents of social chaos and national decline. The conflict between the Catholic Church and the Republic (rather than, as is often stated, the State) was a fundamental element of French politics and the words clerical and anti-clerical became synonyms for Right and Left, terms which themselves date from the Revolution. At various times, violent conflicts have broken out between supporters and opponents of the legacy of the Revolution, with each side claiming that the other was in some sense 'betraying' France. The most famous of these was the Dreyfus Affair (1894–1906) – in its origin a banal miscarriage of justice arising out of a spy scandal – that split the political nation in two and led to the separation of Church and State. It is significant that after France's military defeat in 1940 by Nazi Germany, political power passed to Marshal Pétain who believed that the republican creed of 'liberty, equality and fraternity' was responsible for the collapse. Even today, some of the supporters of the Front National of Jean Marie Le Pen continue to be hostile to the Revolution and to hold an annual day of atonement for its crimes (see Chapter 8).

Thus, in contrast to America in 1776 (or Britain in 1688), the Revolution failed to establish a consensual myth around itself. Political opponents were divided not simply over questions of economic policy and social reform but over basic principles of constitutional form. Should France be a monarchy, an empire, or a republic? And just because constitutional politics were so important, regimes themselves were always vulnerable. The overthrow of the monarchy in 1792 was quickly followed by the overthrow of the parliamentary Republic that replaced it. After further upheavals, Napoleon Bonaparte established a plebiscitary republic in 1799 and then an Empire. The latter lasted until 1814/15 when it was overthrown as a result of military defeat. Between 1815 and 1870 the identical cycle of parliamentary monarchy, republic, empire reoccurred.

In the twentieth century, the prospects of a restoration of the monarchy have disappeared, though there is still a pretender to the throne, the Comte de Paris. Yet the fact that there have been four regimes since January 1940 demonstrates that part of France's political tradition long remained a tradition of revolution. Each regime has had to face a group of irreconcilable opponents ready at any moment to overturn the existing order. The riots that gripped France in 1968, and severely shook President de Gaulle's authority, seemed at the time evidence that the revolutionary virus was still alive.

Like Hayward, most commentators regard the revolutionary demon as having been exorcised from French politics. Yet the consensus around the Fifth Republic (see Chapter 2) does not mean that the constitution is venerated as a sacred text. Constitutions everywhere originate as devices to entrench the victory of a political faction; in France it sometimes seems as if they remain so. French political discourse uses the terms *pouvoir* (power) or *régime* where we would use the more neutral term government, and sometimes distinguishes between those who exercise formal authority (the *pays légal*) and the people (the *pays réel*)

What kind of democracy?

A legacy of the Revolution that helps to explain the constitutional instability we have just noted is that different lessons could be derived from it about the proper organisation of political – and also social – power. The central message of the revolution was that sovereignty resides with the People of France who collectively form the French Nation. The problem is that this says nothing about *how* sovereignty should be organised. It was all very well to talk about power to the people; but where, and in what areas, was that power to operate?

There were a number of answers to this question. One group of revolutionaries sought a socially egalitarian Republic in which private property was to be subordinated to collective needs by a process of forcible expropriation. This group had little influence at the time. But its radicalism inspired later generations of activists on the French – and European – left who believed that political liberty was a sham unless it was accompanied by wholesale socialisation of property. In our own time the French Communist Party has been the inheritor of this tradition. Another political tradition to emerge out of the Revolution is *Jacobinism*. The fame – or notoriety – of Jacobinism is due to its identification with the revolutionary leader Maximilian Robespierre who believed in the need to impose an egalitarian Republic of virtue on the French people and used Terror as a conscious weapon of political salvation. The Jacobins were not in favour of the wholesale expropriation of private property; but they did assert the power of the People against the existing ruling class.

In time, the heirs of Jacobinism came to be identified with the institutionalisation of 'citizen power' in an all-powerful National Assembly composed of the elected representatives of the nation. Jacobin theory argued that all other political and social organisations – government, local authorities, courts – were necessarily subordinate to the National Assembly. Hence the 'republican' concept of power insisted on the sovereignty of the National Assembly – the virtuous Republic was one where the legislature ruled supreme in the name of the People. The Third (1875–1940) and Fourth (1946–58) Republics are known as *régimes d'assemblée* and were characterised by the moral and political pre-eminence of the elected representatives over a weak Executive. Only this system was seen as being compatible with the rights of man and the citizen proclaimed in 1789. As recently as 1962 a veteran member of parliament, speaking in – and of – the National Assembly, said 'Here, and nowhere else, is France'.

Apart from Robespierre, the most celebrated figure to emerge from the Revolution is Napoleon Bonaparte, the Corsican adventurer who in 1804 crowned himself Emperor of France. Napoleon is, of course, better known for his authoritarian rule and for his attempt to assert French hegemony throughout Europe via the series of wars he waged against the other powers rather than for any concerns with the rights of men and citizens. Yet, formally at least, the legitimacy of his rule was based on the support of the People. What came to be known as *Bonapartism* or *Caesarism* or, in the Fifth Republic, as plebiscitary democracy argued that France needed strong government and that this could only be provided by a leader. The latter's authority derived not from parliamentary assemblies but from periodic plebiscites in which the Nation directly expressed its support or disapproval of his actions. In this system the role of the legislature was severely curtailed; it was seen as the instrument whereby warring factions weakened national unity.

What we see in France's constitutional traditions are two opposing concepts of how a democratic state should be organised. Right and Left came to be defined in large part around one or other of the two traditions, with the Right being in favour of an Executive-led system and the Left arguing that the only true democracy was a parliamentary Republic. This led many observers to talk, as recently as the 1970s, of there being a 'war of the Republics'. Supporters of parliamentarism – known as Republicans – regarded strong government as inherently tyrannical, while believers in strong government denounced the feebleness and instability that resulted from the *régime d'assemblée*. Each side could point to the vices of the other. Republicans denounced the authoritarian regime of the Second Empire (1852–70), their critics the weakness of the ninety-eight governments that held office (rather than power) during the sixty-five years of the Third Republic.

The place of the State in French politics

French political traditions are conflictual in that they have lacked the near consensus over the proper shape of constitutional government that has been a characteristic of British politics. Yet there is one area of public power in which otherwise opposing forces have often been in agreement, and that is in the belief that France's security and success require the existence of a strong and centralised state.

The word State is ubiquitous in French politics in a way that it is not in the United Kingdom, or the United States, both of which are sometimes described as having a 'Stateless' culture. The term conveys the idea of a coherent and self-confident institution responsible for the proper ordering of society. The famous phrase of Louis XIV 'I am the State' (*'L'état c'est moi'*) expressed the monarchic idea that all power was concentrated in the person of the king. The significance of the French Revolution was that although the opposing sides disagreed, as we have seen, about the institutional location of sovereignty, they were largely at one over the need for a powerful, and unitary, State. Why was this so – and why does it remain so? Two reasons are important:

1. The famous political philosopher Jean Jacques Rousseau put forward the thesis of the General Will. He argued that modern society could only operate properly if its members abandoned selfish individualism for a unity of purpose based on their shared citizenship. This universalist view of the national community helps explain why parties and pressure groups have often been regarded with suspicion in France as enemies of the General Will and why, to British and American observers, France lacks a pluralist political culture based on the legitimacy of diversity (see Chapter 9). But it also explains the high status accorded to the State as the agent, and the realiser, of national goals. There has, for example, been less opposition in France than in the United States and Britain to a dynamic role for the State in economic, and particularly industrial, management (see Chapter 5).

2. A second reason for the importance of the State is the belief that without it France would fall apart. The construction of present day France took place over centuries as a result of action from the centre and it was argued that without a strong state the nation might disintegrate. Governments of all political shades have feared the centrifugal tendencies at work within French society and have believed that only a strong state can counteract them. As President Pompidou said in 1970 'For over a thousand years France has owed its existence to the State, a State that alone can protect it not only from external threats but from internal rivalries'. Anyone who visits France will know that it is a country of great geographical and cultural variety. Successive regimes regarded regionalism as subversive of national unity and sought to suppress the expression of regionalist identities. Over the last ten years, as Chapter 6 notes, regional political institutions have been created and regional initiatives encouraged. Yet it is significant that as recently as 1990 the Constitutional Council declared unconstitutional a law that, in attempting to deal with the endemic separatist tensions in Corsica, referred to 'the

Corsican people' as a component part of the French people. For the Council, there could only be one French people.

Thus the second reason for France having a statist political culture is based on a justifiable pessimism about the solidity of its political institutions and a, less warranted, fear of the fragility of its nationhood. This pessimism contributed to the other characteristic of French statism which is the centralised nature of government. Ever since the Revolution, France has been viewed as a country in which the Centre closely supervises, when it does not actually direct, other political organisations, and notably local government. France is said to have local administration rather than local government (see Chapter 6).

The symbol of French centralisation is the prefect, an official of central government whose task is to ensure that local authorities comply with its commands. The corps of prefects was created by Napoleon. But the significant point about them is that they had existed, under a different name, before the Revolution – and also during the rule of the Jacobin republicans. To this day the words Jacobinism and Bonapartism signify a commitment to centralisation and a fear of the disintegrating effects of devolution.

There have always been critics of the power of the State in France. It is also easy to show that in its everyday workings, the central administration is much less effective and unitary than the myth of the State would suggest. The Third Republic, France's longest lasting regime since the Revolution, owed its survival in part to its rulers' use of the State machine to protect a socio-political order based on the interests of the 'small man'. At the present time, important changes in the power relations between central and local government are taking place and French membership of the European Community has obvious implications for the authority of the State. Yet the fact remains that the State does have an important symbolic importance in French politics and that, for all their criticism of its inefficiencies and authoritarianism, the French have had high expectations of it. France is still a much-governed nation and its senior officials

- the *hauts fonctionnaires* – have at times (including the Fifth Republic) enjoyed high status as a professionally competent elite, seen as possessing more expertise and a stronger 'sense of the State' than the elected politicians (see Chapter 5).

The rights of man and the rule of law

The French Revolution proclaimed as its goal the realisation of the rights of man and the citizen. To many observers, however, France has seemed a country in which individual liberties have been rather poorly protected in law. Feminists argue that the Revolution retarded rather than advanced the cause of emancipation – women in France did not receive the vote until 1944. More generally it has been claimed that the historic concern with the legitimacy of the *origins* of public power leads to an indifference to its uses – and abuses. According to this argument, the negative liberty of the individual to do what he or she wants is lacking in a political tradition that asserts the State's ability to realise a (mythical) national unity. In the 1970s the British conservative Enoch Powell wrote that the French State was the most powerful institution in Europe outside the Soviet Union.

One sign of the apparent indifference to individual liberties is the rather weak protection afforded to private citizens against the State. It is alleged that the courts are unduly subservient to the will of the Executive and that France lacks a tradition of judicial independence (the police, by contrast, sometimes appear to be a law unto themselves). Allegations of political interference in the judicial process are a constant theme in political debate and until the Fifth Republic France lacked any institution capable, like the United States Supreme Court, of controlling the constitutionality of the exercise of power (see Chapters 2 and 5).

These shortcomings are easy to understand, if not to justify, when one considers the traumas France has experienced in the twentieth century. Such dramatic events as the military collapse of 1940, the colonial wars in Indo-China (1947–54) and Algeria (1954–62) and the mass demonstrations of May 1968 were bound to put great pressure on the system. Governments were torn between the republican duty to defend democracy and the need to defend the regime against subversion. Their problems were made greater by the fact that the fragility of regimes meant that yesterday's subversives could be tomorrow's rulers.

The impact of war

For most of the twentieth century, the United Kingdom (with the exception of Ireland) and the United States have had positive views of their political systems. In France this is not the case. Perhaps the most dramatic evidence of the 'failure' of French politics came in 1940. Accounts of British politics emphasise the role of the Second World War, and particularly the 'finest hour' of 1940, in consolidating a sense of national pride and confidence in the merits of the country's political institutions and in creating the conditions for the post-war consensus. Parliamentary democracy was not only morally superior to anything else on offer, it was also, as the outcome of the war showed, more efficient.

The year 1940 was also a decisive moment in France's political evolution – but for wholly different reasons. It witnessed not the country's 'finest hour' but rather its rapid, total and humiliating defeat at the hands of Nazi Germany. Only six weeks separate the invasion of 10 May from the armistice signed with the German authorities which resulted in Nazi Occupation of much of France (including the capital Paris). But even more important than the military defeat was the political upheaval that accompanied it. With the military collapse of 1940 the bulk of the political class – and indeed of the population – lost confidence not simply in the politicians of the Third Republic, but in the values of liberal democracy. The country turned to a legendary former soldier, the eighty-four year old Marshal Pétain, to save them from the consequences of defeat.

Pétain, like Churchill, was a hero figure. Unlike Churchill, he was not a believer in parliamentary liberalism and he was firmly convinced that the defeat showed the rottenness of the

Third Republic, and of the republican traditions it espoused. Pétain lent his authority to all those who argued that France needed an authoritarian (if not necessarily fascist) regime based on the rejection of the principles of 1789. The result was that on 10 July 1940 the Third Republic was replaced by the so-called French State (Etat Français) which has been known ever since as the Vichy regime (Vichy was the spa town where the transfer of power took place and where Pétain, the new head of state, installed his government). The institutions of the Third Republic – parliament and presidency – were abolished and so too, in a decision of great symbolic importance, was the ideological device of the French Revolution – liberty, equality, fraternity.

Pétain's goal was to reshape France along conservative and hierarchical goals – he sought to create national unity by purging the political culture of its democratic and egalitarian poisons. Instead of uniting the country, however, the Vichy regime intensified its divisions. From the beginning, some French men and women rejected the armistice, and the collaboration with Nazi Germany that ensued, and embarked on a policy of Resistance. The most celebrated of the dissenters was General de Gaulle (1890–1970) who launched the Free French movement in a BBC broadcast from London on 18 June 1940. Though few people in mainland France – or in the (unconquered) French Empire – initially joined the Resistance, it showed the existence of a dissenting politics. By 1943 an important Resistance movement was in place inside and outside France.

The motives that led French people to oppose the Vichy regime differed. Some were outraged by what they regarded as Pétain's abandonment of national independence in its policy of collaboration with Germany; others remained loyal to the democratic principles of the Republic and were disgusted by such features of Vichy rule as the persecution of the Jews; many young men joined the armed Resistance to avoid being sent to work in German factories. An important addition to Resistance strength came in June 1941 when Hitler invaded Soviet Russia and the French Communist Party threw itself into the struggle against the Germans and their Vichy puppets.

Pétain's regime did not lose all support – by early 1944 a brutal civil war was raging between Resistance groups and the Vichy forces, who were supported by the Germans. Nor is it the case that the whole population can be divided into resisters and collaborators, since the preoccupation of many ordinary people was simply survival. But Vichy failed in its three principal goals of sparing France further involvement in the war; protecting the authority of the State; and destroying the influence of the Left, in particular the Communist Party. In the summer of 1944, a major land war was being fought on French soil, the authority of Pétain's government had virtually collapsed and the Communist Party was emerging as the most powerful party in the country. In August Pétain and the remnants of his government were carted off to Germany with the retreating Nazi armies and General de Gaulle entered Paris in triumph. Though fractions of the national territory were not freed from German control until Spring 1945, by the end of 1944 France was a liberated country.

The failed modernisation of French politics 1945–58

At the end of the war, Vichy's leading figures – including the eighty-nine year old Pétain – were put on trial and condemned to long terms of imprisonment or to death. Thousands of other collaborators suffered legal – and in many cases extra-legal – punishment. General de Gaulle headed a provisional government containing members of all the established parties, including the Communists. The new government swiftly established its authority over a country that had recently been near to civil war and enacted a series of major social and economic reforms, including the establishment of a welfare state and the nationalisation of the clearing banks and insurance companies.

The experience of Vichy shattered the appeal of counter-revolutionary conservatism, which lost all authority through its association with the Nazi Occupation. Yet if a Republic was henceforth the only legitimate constitutional structure, it soon became clear that a return to the discredited political system of pre-war France was as unacceptable as Pétain's Etat Français.

Ninety-five per cent of the electorate (which for the first time included women) voted against the restoration of the Third Republic in the referendum of October 1945 and opted instead for a new constitution to be drawn up by a Constituent Assembly and ratified by referendum. The three dominant political parties of liberated France – the Communists (PCF), The Socialists (SFIO), and the Christian Democrats (MRP) – were all in favour of the establishment of a Fourth Republic, and so too was General de Gaulle.

The Fourth Republic duly came into being in November 1946, after long parliamentary debates and the rejection by the electorate of an initial text. Enshrined in the new constitution was the republican principle of the supreme authority of the democratically elected National Assembly, to which the government was accountable. The experience of Vichy – and also of de Gaulle who resigned as head of the provisional government in 1946 – had heightened fears of the threat to democracy posed by personalised power (*le pouvoir personnel*). Thus the president of the Republic had a largely ceremonial and advisory role. The constitution makers hoped that the chronic governmental instability of the Third Republic could be eliminated and attempted to strengthen the constitutional position, and administrative resources, of the prime minister. Yet the chief prop of the new system was to be a simplified, and disciplined, party system, which would provide coherent governmental majorities in the National Assembly. In the immediate post-war elections, the PCF, SFIO and MRP between them gained seventy-five per cent of the votes and eighty per cent of the parliamentary seats. Here lay the basis for ordered parliamentary government. All three parties co-operated in government after de Gaulle's resignation in January 1946. They appeared willing to make the new system work and shared a commitment to economic and social reform. Thus it appeared that France, like Britain, might have its post-war consensus.

We should not underestimate the reconstruction that occurred in France during the Fourth Republic. The so-called *trente glorieuses* (thirty glorious years) of economic growth began in these years; after years of stagnation France's economy and population embarked on a long period of sustained growth. Industrial production soared, the birth rate reached levels not seen since the Revolution and the urbanisation of a hitherto rural society got under way. A long tradition of protectionism was abandoned as France joined the emerging institutions of European economic co-operation, the Coal and Steel Community (1951) and the European Economic Community (1957). Fourth Republic governments took the important, and durable, foreign policy initiatives of committing France to the Atlantic Alliance (1949) and to a policy of reconciliation with the hereditary enemy, Germany (see Chapter 10).

Yet the problem of political instability remained unsolved. Governments came and went with the same frequency as before the war so that between 1946 and 1958 France had twenty-five ministries and eighteen prime ministers. Only one government lasted more than a year and a number fell within a day or two of appointment. At its foundation, the Republic had lacked mass support – it was voted in by nine million votes to eight million, with over eight million, including de Gaulle, abstaining. After the 1951 general elections, the two largest parties in the National Assembly (Communist and Gaullist) were both committed to the overthrow of the political system. Even the pro-system parties were internally divided as old political conflicts – for example between Catholic and anti-clerical parties – re-emerged and new ones (decolonisation) appeared. All governments were unstable coalitions likely to succumb at any moment to internal divisions. In 1953 thirteen ballots were necessary before Parliament could vote a new president of the Republic, and in the last year of the Fourth Republic France was without a government for an average of one day in four. Alexander Werth, a distinguished foreign analyst, wrote in 1955 of 'the lost battle for the New France'. Three years later, in May 1958, the Fourth Republic collapsed, the victim, like its predecessor, of a challenge from the military. The difference is that, whereas in 1940 the German army acted as the catalyst for regime change, in 1958 it was French soldiers that did so out of anger at the regime's failure to 'win' the war against the Algerian nationalists. The failure of the Fourth Republic seemed complete; and its reputation has never recovered.

Governmental instability and a fragmented party system were not on their own enough to bring the regime down. The Communist Party was unable (if such indeed was its aim), to overthrow the system and de Gaulle failed to capitalise on his initial successes. By 1954 his political movement, the Rassemblement pour la France (RPF), was dead and de Gaulle had abandoned political life. The example of post-war Italy shows that a regime can survive in a multi-party system and with chronic governmental weakness.

The 1958 crisis and the end of the Fourth Republic

What the Fourth Republic could not resolve was the crisis of decolonisation that raged in Algeria from 1954 onwards. It should be noted that other European countries also faced the upsurge of nationalist movements in their empires and that the regime was able to survive, albeit after a long and bloody conflict, the loss of Indo-China in 1954 and the granting of independence to Morocco and Tunisia. Algeria, however, was different. Over the years many Europeans had settled in Algeria and they, and their political allies on the mainland, fiercely resisted any separation of the ties that bound them to France. Once the Algerian independence movement, FLN (Front de Libération Nationale) launched its military campaign, the French army engaged it in a fierce, and brutal, struggle. Army leaders were determined to prevent another humiliation of the sort that had occurred in Indo-China and many of them were also convinced that the independence movement was part of a worldwide movement of communist subversion.

The problem for the governments of the Fourth Republic was that they were distrusted not only by the European settlers but also by the army commanders who felt that Paris was ready, out of weakness, to betray the cause of French Algeria. Whether this fear was justified is irrelevant; the point is that it was widely held. Once the government appeared ready, in Spring 1958, to yield to hostile international pressure to negotiate with the FLN, the situation boiled over. The Europeans in Algeria rebelled and were supported by the Army.

France thus experienced a crisis in civil–military relations that developed into a full-scale breakdown of political authority. The regime was destroyed by the inability of its leaders – president of the Republic René Coty, prime minister Pierre Pflimlin, and the party leaders – to face down a rebellion of those who had lost confidence in the system. As in 1940, political authority resided with a leader who stood outside – and against – the existing political system. That leader was General de Gaulle who offered himself as the saviour of his country in the same way that Marshal Pétain had done eighteen years earlier. De Gaulle's wartime record as the incarnation of French patriotism appealed to those who feared the loss of French Algeria. But the fact that he had restored the Republic in 1944 meant he was also acceptable to many politicians of the Centre and the non-communist Left who regarded him as the only man capable of saving France from the real threat of a military, or Communist, coup.

On 1 June 1958 a majority of the members of the National Assembly voted to accept de Gaulle as prime minister. In so doing they signed the death warrant of the Fourth Republic, since de Gaulle, like Pétain, was determined to use a military crisis to create a new constitutional framework for French politics. From his determination emerged the Fifth Republic and the present political system.

Further reading

J. Hayward, *Governing France, the One and Indivisible French Republic.* London: Weidenfeld and Nicolson (1983).

J. F. McMillan, *Twentieth Century France, Politics and Society 1898– 1901.* London: Edward Arnold (1992).

2
The constitutional settlement of the Fifth Republic

The Fifth Republic was created in 1958. We have seen that its origins lie in the inability of its predecessor to reconcile effective government with parliamentary institutions at a time of crisis. Faced with the pressures of the Algerian war, and beset by multipartyism of a conflicting nature, the authority of the existing institutions collapsed. There was no mass uprising in mainland France against the Fourth Republic; but neither was there any sign that the electorate felt any loyalty to it. The sixty-seven year old de Gaulle was welcomed back to power as the heroic leader who could somehow 'solve' the Algerian crisis while preserving democratic government in France.

If the majority of the French people were primarily concerned with Algeria, the new prime minister was determined to use the authority he had acquired to install a new institutional order. Though careful to ensure that he was constitutionally appointed by the National Assembly, de Gaulle rejected absolutely the legitimacy of the Fourth Republic. He was convinced that France's political difficulties sprang from the destructive influence of the political parties and that this in turn resulted from the excessive power of the National Assembly within the system. Redressing the constitutional balance in order to strengthen the authority of government was the core of his project.

Even though a number of constitutional experts and ministers worked on the text of the new constitution, de Gaulle is correctly seen as the 'founding father' of the Fifth Republic. Immediately after his appointment, he got the National Assembly to pass a law which gave his government power to draw up a new constitution. In September 1958 a draft constitution was presented to the French people who were invited to give their verdict by a referendum. On 28 September 79 per cent of the voters registered their approval in the referendum; six days later, on 4 October, the constitution was officially promulgated. Elections for the new National Assembly took place in November and in January 1959 de Gaulle became the first president of the Fifth Republic.

The process of constitution-making reveals an important element in de Gaulle's intentions: unlike in 1945/6, there was to be no role for an elected Constituent Assembly, whose membership reflected the strength of the political parties. Though some party leaders were members of de Gaulle's government and other prominent parliamentarians sat on a Constitutional Consultative Committee, the constitution was not first submitted to the National Assembly for its approval. Instead, it was ratified over the heads of the parties through a direct appeal to the electorate in a referendum. This concern to protect decision-taking from Parliament and parties was a harbinger of the future constitutional practice of the Fifth Republic.

The constitutional principles of the Fifth Republic

1. Republicanism

In 1958 de Gaulle was attacked by his enemies inside and outside France as a political reactionary, if not actually as an aspiring dictator, and he was compared with such figures as Louis XIV, Napoleon Bonaparte and Napoleon III, and the Spanish dictator General Franco. Some opponents, including the future president of the Republic François Mitterrand, denounced the circumstances in which de Gaulle returned to power as a *coup d'état* of the sort that Louis Napoleon Bonaparte had engineered in 1851 against the democratically elected Second Republic. De Gaulle's family background was Catholic and monarchist, his career was that of an army officer and he was imbued with a belief in his personal destiny to rule France. The author of a remarkably prescient pre-war study of political leadership, *Le Fil de l'Epée*, he had regarded himself since 1940 as incarnating national legitimacy, a fact which explains why he had no scruples in allowing his supporters in 1958 to engage in anti-constitutional activities. He believed that he possessed a personal relationship with the French people that transcended constitutional niceties. It is significant that even after 1959 he preferred to be addressed as 'Mon Général' rather than as 'monsieur le President' and that he would have preferred the Constitution to refer to the 'Head of State' rather than the 'President of the Republic'.

De Gaulle viewed political action in heroic terms and exercised charismatic authority over his closest supporters, who regarded him with near religious veneration. Yet if his political style was authoritarian, his conception of the origin of governmental authority was democratic. He accepted that in the modern world universal suffrage was the only legitimate source of political power and that the new constitution must acknowledge the principles of the 1789 Revolution and the symbols of France's republican tradition. The draft constitution was presented to the electorate on 4 September 1958 – the anniversary of the date on which the Third Republic came into being in 1870, after the overthrow of Napoleon III. The preamble to the constitution sets out its commitment to the 1789 Declaration of the Rights of Man and the Citizen, and to the social rights proclaimed in the preamble of the 1946 Constitution. Article 2 declares the new Republic's attachment to the symbols of the Republic – the tricolor flag, the *Marseillaise* national anthem, the principles of liberty, equality and fraternity and the separation of Church and State. Article 89 states that the republican form of government cannot be altered and reserves to Parliament the power of constitutional amendment.

There is another crucial way in which the text of the Fifth Republic respects the principles of republicanism. This is the assertion, in the constitutional law of 2 June 1958 and in Article 20 of the final text, that the Government is responsible for its actions to Parliament. The principle of ministerial responsibility – that a government cannot continue in office without the confidence of the democratically elected National Assembly – was fundamental to French Republicanism and de Gaulle would not have gained parliamentary assent for his return to power unless he had accepted it. The Constitution also provides for an upper house, the Senate, modelled on that of the Third Republic, and guarantees the right of political parties to organise freely and to compete for votes.

2. The rights of President and Government

If the constitution of the Fifth Republic incorporates elements of France's republican heritage, its provisions nevertheless depart from constitutional traditions that had developed since 1875. They do so in two separate but related ways, both of which reflect de Gaulle's determination to re-establish the authority of government and prevent the 'confusion of powers' that he regarded as the besetting sin of the Third and Fourth Republics.

Thus the constitution aims to put an end to the perversion of parliamentary government known as the *régime d'assemblée*, in which the combination of a dominant National Assembly and a fragmented party system made stable government impossible. To achieve this separation of powers, a battery of measures (outlined in Chapter 5) defines the working relationship between legislature and executive in ways that are highly restrictive of Parliament's traditional right to determine its own agenda and procedures, and make it much more difficult for a government to be overthrown. Parliament also lost its monopoly over the law-making function by the introduction of a procedure for legislation by referendum and by the creation of a Constitutional Council (see below) charged with supervising the constitutionality of laws voted by the National Assembly. These two provisions mark a clear break with the republican tradition of parliamentary sovereignty. So too did the constitutional provision (Article 6) depriving Parliament of its traditional right to elect the President of the Republic. By establishing an electoral college of some 80,000 members (mainly local councillors) to choose the President, the 1958 text emphasised that Parliament was no longer the only source of Executive authority.

The other side to the weakening of Parliament was the constitutional affirmation of the rights of government. These rights run like a thread through the text of the Constitution and can be explained by France's recent political history, a history in which, it should be remembered, de Gaulle had been intimately involved. He had briefly been a government minister during the military collapse of 1940 and was appalled by the lack of authority of the Executive, and in particular of the then president of the Republic, Albert Lebrun, at a moment of supreme national crisis. He believed that the failure of the Third and Fourth Republics to acknowledge the importance of a strong presidency to national security was the cause of the disasters that had befallen France in recent decades. Hence an effective presidency was to be the *clé de voûte* or corner-stone of the new institutional order.

A number of constitutional provisions assert the authority of the head of state. Article 5 makes the president the guarantor of national independence (the implicit reference to 1940 is clear) and the protector – through his arbitration (*arbitrage*) – of the proper functioning of public powers and of the continuity of the State. Article 15 makes him head of the armed forces and Article 64 the guarantor of the independence of the judiciary and president of the High Council of the Magistrature. Other articles give the president the institutional resources and weapons that can turn formal authority into real power by enabling him to influence a given political situation. Thus the Fifth Republic president possesses prerorative powers, that is to say powers that do not need to be countersigned by any other State official. The most important of them are the appointment of the prime minister (Article 8), the right to dissolve (within certain limits) the National Assembly (Article 12), the right to declare a state of emergency and rule by decree (Article 16), and the right to nominate three members of the Constitutional Council (Article 61).

The Constitution makers' concern to strengthen the authority of the president of the Republic should not, however, be misinterpreted. We have already seen that the republican principle of the accountability of government to legislature was fundamental to the agreement reached in 1958 between de Gaulle and the politicians. The Fifth Republic Constitution is thus parliamentary in character. Article 20 states that it is the government – and not therefore the president – which decides and implements the policy of the Nation and runs the civil service and the armed forces. By stating that the government is accountable to the National Assembly, it emphasises the parliamentary nature of governmental authority. Article 21 establishes a prime minister to direct the work of government, to be responsible for national defence, to implement laws and to make appointments to civil and military posts.

Thus the constitution creates a system in which both president of the Republic on the one hand and prime minister and government on the other have defined functions. We have explained why this should be so; that it was so led many commentators to criticise the confusion at the heart of the 1958 text and to describe it, as Vincent Wright does, as a fudge (though compromise might be a better word). Yet the letter of the Constitution certainly implies a system in which prime minister and government 'rule' the country and the president of the Republic 'referees' the political game. Only in exceptional circumstances (the declaration of a state of emergency, the dissolution of the National Assembly) do presidential decisions not require the countersignature of the 'responsible' prime minister. Michel Debré, de Gaulle's principal collaborator in drawing up the Constitution and the first prime minister of the Fifth Republic, was known to admire the British system of parliamentary government in which prime minister and government enjoyed a co-operative, rather than conflictual relationship with the House of Commons to which they were responsible. Nothing in the 1958 texts stops prime ministers, supported by a majority of the National Assembly, using their constitutional powers to determine national policy over the head of the President.

The presidentialising of government

It is necessary to stress the non-presidential nature of the 1958 Constitution for a simple, but essential, reason. In the decades following its establishment, the Fifth Republic came to be dominated by the Presidency: the occupant of the presidential palace (the Elysée) exercised the reality of power in the same way that the British prime minister or West German chancellor are seen to do (see Chapter 3). The Fifth Republic presidents (Charles de Gaulle 1959–69; Georges Pompidou 1969–74; Valéry Giscard d'Estaing (1974–81); and François Mitterrand 1981–) have dominated French politics since 1958. Only on two occasions – from 1986 to 1988 and since April 1993 – have prime ministers been able to determine the main areas of policy. For the rest of the time, prime ministers and their governments have resembled chiefs of staff rather than leaders, subordinate to the president and holding office only so long as the latter wishes.

Thus to understand the constitutional settlement of the Fifth Republic we need to explain the emergence of a constitutional practice that converted a 'two headed' executive into one where, except in the circumstances of 'cohabitation' defined below, the president is in command.

The Constitutional Crisis of 1962

In 1959 de Gaulle chose the presidency rather than the premiership as the basis of his power, thereby indicating his view of where true political authority lay. As he wrote in his memoirs 'henceforth, the head of State is really at the head of affairs, really responsible for France and the Republic ... every important decision and all authority derives from him' (Hayward 1993, p. 23). In the new Republic, politics continued to be dominated by the Algerian war of independence and de Gaulle's presidential authority was buttressed by the fact that he alone seemed capable of managing a highly dangerous situation. The new National Assembly did not dare to challenge him, and his prime minister, Michel Debré, could also be relied on to remain loyal. Between 1960 and 1962 a series of referenda gave massive backing to de Gaulle's policy of self-determination for Algeria, a policy that culminated in full independence for Algeria in Summer 1962.

De Gaulle's success in ending the Algerian war led to the decisive event in the constitutional evolution of the regime. With the Algerian crisis over, the coalition that had backed de Gaulle in 1958 fell apart. Its non-Gaullist members felt that it was now safe to challenge the presidentialist style – and hence the president – of the Fifth Republic and to revert to a more traditional system. De Gaulle for his part was determined to resist any return to the hated *régime des partis* of the Fourth Republic. The result was a head-on confrontation between President and Parliament. Four years earlier, at the height of the Algerian crisis, both sides had wanted to avoid such a clash for fear of the consequences that might follow. Now they felt free to confront each other.

The crisis was precipitated by de Gaulle's decision to invite the French people to approve by referendum a constitutional amendment providing for the direct election of the presidency. This was a direct challenge to the French republican tradition which ever since Louis Bonaparte's coup of 1851 had held that a directly elected president signalled the end of political liberty. De Gaulle compounded the offence by using a referendum procedure (Article 11) for the amendment that bypassed Parliament and was held by almost all constitutional experts to be illegal. The National Assembly responded by passing a vote of censure on de Gaulle's government, which was thereby forced to resign. De Gaulle promptly exercised his constitutional right to dissolve the National Assembly and instructed his defeated government to stay in office until after the legislative elections that were to follow the referendum.

At stake were two concepts of the institutional future of the Fifth Republic. Aware of his own mortality (he had just survived a serious assassination attempt), de Gaulle argued that the Fifth Republic presidency, and hence governmental stability, would only be safe if future holders of the office possessed sufficient authority. How could a system created for an extraordinary leader continue to operate when ordinary politicians took over? Given that de Gaulle's personal authority could not, by definition, be transferred to his successor, the latter's legitimacy as guarantor of the stability of the Republic would only be assured if it was based on universal suffrage. For their part, the political parties held that de Gaulle was seeking to overturn republican democracy and to install an elective despotism based on personal power (*le pouvoir personnel*). They wanted a system in which political authority resided with the government and the National Assembly.

In the October 1962 referendum, 62 per cent of the electorate accepted the principle of a directly elected president. A few weeks later the voters gave de Gaulle a comfortable majority in the elections to the National Assembly.

This was a turning point in the constitutional evolution of the republic. The French political scientist Maurice Duverger summed up the significance of the referendum in a phrase that has become famous: 'the constitutional amendment of 1962 gave the president no new powers – but it gave him power'. Henceforth the electoral legitimacy of the president of the Republic would be equal to that of the National Assembly. In his speeches and press conferences de Gaulle constantly stressed that all Executive powers derived from the presidency and that he was the Nation's guide, (a term he preferred to referee). An ordinance of 1964 gave the president sole responsibility for the decision to use France's independent nuclear deterrent. According to de Gaulle, there was no area of public policy on which the president could not decide, if he chose to do so.

The consolidation of Presidential power

The year 1962 is thus a crucial date. But what Duverger did not say in his analysis of the significance of the 1962 referendum is that the other provisions of the 1958 constitution remained in place. The prime minister and government continued to govern, to introduce bills into Parliament and to be responsible to the National Assembly, which continued to vote the laws. Hence an account of the presidentialising of the political system of the Fifth Republic needs to look at the conventions that came to shape the relationship between the head of state and the other governing institutions.

Three factors explain the buttressing of the presidency:

1. De Gaulle's prime ministers accepted a status which made them agents of presidential power, rather than rivals to it. Debré (1959–62), Pompidou (1962–68) and Couve de Murville (1968–69) were all 'unconditionalists' in that they were close political, and personal, associates of de Gaulle. They recognised that their authority derived from his and they never attempted while in office to organise political, or party, opinion against his decisions even when they disagreed with them. They also accepted, although the Constitution did not state this, that their tenure of office depended on the president's will rather than any decision of the National Assembly and that if he wanted them to go, then go they would.

    After de Gaulle's departure in 1969, his two successors, Georges Pompidou (1969–74) and Valéry Giscard d'Estaing (1974–81) continued to regard the presidency as dominant and the prime minister as the agent of its will. Pompidou in particular asserted his authority in a very direct fashion in 1972 by dismissing a prime minister (Chaban–Delmas) only six weeks after the latter had gained a substantial vote of confidence in the National Assembly. We shall see later that the prime minister in the Fifth Republic is much more than an American vice-president; but only in special circumstances is he or she a rival to the head of state.

2. The transformation of the party system in the National Assembly. In 1962, a presidentialist majority was returned to the National Assembly. The Gaullist Party and its allies (known collectively as the Majority) saw their role as providing disciplined support for the president and his government. Thus the National Assembly, for the first time in the history of France's Republics, came to resemble the British House of Commons: its role was to support, and not to de-stabilise, government. This change was of great importance in shaping the constitutional culture of the Fifth Republic.

    Once again, de Gaulle's departure did not change the situation. It is true that Giscard d'Estaing had more difficulty than his two predecessors in maintaining a disciplined parliamentary majority, particularly after 1978. But overall presidential control of the Assembly remained intact due to the fact that both presidency and National Assembly were controlled by the same political Majority. Only one Fifth Republic government (Pompidou, 1962) has been defeated by a censure motion.

3. The acceptance by the Opposition of the new institutional order. The election to the presidency of the Socialist François Mitterrand in 1981 marks an important stage in the consolidation of the presidency. Mitterrand had opposed de Gaulle's return to power in 1958 and thereafter constantly criticised what he regarded as the abuses of democracy inherent in constitutionally irresponsible presidentialism. The coalition of Socialists and Communists that he headed in 1981 was in some sense the heir to the old republican tradition, described in Chapter 1, that viewed the National Assembly as the legitimate home of sovereignty. Both Socialists and Communists could be expected to have a more extensive view of their rights than their conservative opponents and to be less automatically deferential to the Executive.

Yet what the Mitterrand presidency really demonstrates is the extent to which the French Left, as well as the Right, had adapted to the institutional culture of the Fifth Republic. It too made the presidency the basis of its power. Mitterrand declared that 'the institutions of the Fifth Republic were not fashioned with me in mind . . . but they suit me very well'. After his election, he showed his determination to use the full range of presidential powers by dissolving the (right-wing dominated) National Assembly elected in 1978 and holding fresh elections.

The Socialists won an absolute majority of the seats. Mitterrand thus obtained the supportive parliamentary majority which is the corner-stone of presidential power. Ten years later, in 1991, Mitterrand gave a blunt demonstration of presidential primacy by sacking, with only a few hours' notice, his popular prime minister Michel Rocard. Another way in which Mitterrand has accepted the constitutional practice which he earlier denounced is in his acknowledgement that Article 11 can be used for constitutional reform. The fact that the Socialist Majority in the National Assembly saw its prime role as giving support to the president's governments indicates the extent to which constitutional conventions have evolved in the Fifth Republic. Possession of the Elysée Palace is now the key prize in the French political system and the party system organises around it. None of the major parties, with the exception of the fast-declining Communists, advocates the abolition of the direct election of the presidency and presidential elections attract very high turn-outs – 80 per cent in the last three contests.

It is also significant that there have been no constitutional amendments affecting the presidency since 1962, though proposals have been made to reduce the length of the term of office from seven to five years. A constitutional bill providing for a five-year presidency made some headway in 1973 before being abandoned. Towards the end of his second presidency, when his political authority was declining, Mitterrand floated a number of constitutional reforms – including the abolition of Article 16 which allows the presidency to declare a state of emergency and rule by decree – in an attempt to 'democratise' the exercise of presidential power. Nothing has come of them. Mitterrand also reneged on his 1981 commitment to reform the High Council of the Magistrature by declaring his intention to remain its president.

The limits to presidentialism

It can appear that the emergence of a 'presidential' majority in the National Assembly has made the constitutional limitations on the Fifth Republic Presidency irrelevant. The dominance of the presidency is, however, less protected by the Constitution than the record of the last thirty-five years suggests. Political developments since the mid-1980s show that the power of the president depends on a specific set of circumstances which, if removed, can shift the constitutional balance within the Executive in favour of the prime minister and government.

From the beginning of the Fifth Republic, commentators and politicians alike recognised that the 'presidentialist' reading of power depends upon a supportive National Assembly. As the nationally elected leader (the *élu de la nation*), the president claims the right to appoint the government and to determine the content of policy. Yet he governs through a prime minister who is responsible to the National Assembly and his policies can only be implemented by parliamentary legislation. Prime ministers thus become the vital link between presidency and National Assembly. They need to be acceptable to the former who appoints them and to the latter which can overthrow them. Only so long as the majority in the National Assembly is of the same political complexion as the president can the Republic function as its founder – if not its Constitution – intended it to.

But the electoral cycle of the seven-year presidency does not coincide with that of the National Assembly; the latter must be renewed at least every five years. The Achilles' heel of the system, as one Gaullist leader described it, was the possibility that an incumbent president might find himself facing a National Assembly which was controlled by his opponents and which he was unable, for constitutional or political reasons, to dissolve.

What then happens to presidential supremacy, and indeed to constitutional stability, if a 'war of the two majorities' were to take place?

In the legislative elections of 1962, 1967, 1968, 1973, 1978, 1981 and 1988, the president's parliamentary supporters 'won' and so guaranteed his position. But in 1986 and again in 1993 the conservative parties gained control of the National Assembly on a programme of opposition to the record and programme of President Mitterrand. Thus the crisis scenario predicted for Fifth Republic presidentialism came into being: the Head of State no longer controlled the legislature. In such a scenario a number of outcomes are possible.

If the President is prepared to challenge the newly elected Assembly he can:

1. resign his office and fight a new presidential election on his record and his programme;
2. dissolve the newly elected Chamber to try to get a different result;
3. attempt to destabilise the new majority by appointing a prime minister who is not its natural leader but who may be able to command a cross party majority in the National Assembly.

If the president does not wish to challenge the National Assembly he can appoint a government that reflects the new majority and withdraw from policy-making in some areas. Meanwhile he can continue to assert his authority as 'guardian of the Constitution' and the national interest and seek wherever possible to improve his political standing by criticising unpopular government decisions. Alternatively he can simply resign office.

Strategies 1–3 are high risk in that their failure could cause lasting damage to the authority of the presidency by demonstrating its vulnerability to the National Assembly. Hence in both 1986 and 1993 President Mitterrand appointed as prime minister a leader of the conservative coalition, and effectively handed over to him the control of key areas of policy-making.

The arrangement reached in 1986 and 1993 is known

as cohabitation. The extent to which cohabitation protects presidential authority from a hostile National Assembly depends on political circumstances. It worked reasonably well between 1986 and the presidential elections of 1988, because of growing policy convergences between Left and Right, notably in the area of foreign and defence matters, and because of the continuing popularity of Mitterrand and, to a lesser extent, the Socialist Party. The success of cohabitation also reflected the desire of the principal actors involved, Mitterrand and prime minister Chirac, not to weaken the presidency within two years of an election that both hoped to win. After the 1993 elections things were different. Mitterrand was no longer a candidate for a future presidential election, he was much more unpopular than he had been in 1986 and his position *vis-à-vis* the National Assembly and government was correspondingly weaker. He did not attempt, as he had successfully done in 1986, to veto the appointment of particular individuals to key ministries.

Yet it is significant that even when faced with a much weakened opponent in the Elysée, the 1993 conservative government did not immediately attempt to drive him from office. That this should be so reflects the power that the constitution gives to a prime minister who has a solid parliamentary majority when faced with a president who does not – and also the desire of all the major parties to protect the constitutional authority of the presidency. Cohabitation thus demonstrates the flexibility of the constitutional system of the Fifth Republic and its ability to respond to changing political situations.

Constitutional limits to power: the developing role of the Constitutional Council

Article 56 of the 1958 constitution established a Constitutional Council with the task of supervising the regularity of presidential and parliamentary elections and judging the constitutionality of laws voted by the National Assembly before they are promulgated by the government. The Council can also declare whether an international treaty conforms to the Constitution. It is composed of nine members, three of whom are appointed by the president of the Republic and three each by the presidents of the National Assembly and Senate.

We have seen that the creation of the Constitutional Council marks another break with the principle of parliamentary sovereignty. For the first time in the history of the Republics, measures approved by both houses of Parliament can be overturned by another body. There is no appeal against a decision of the Council, other than via a reform of the constitutional provision that motivated it. An observer might conclude that what the constitution makers of the Fifth Republic sought was some version of the judicial control over the political process exercised by the United States Supreme Court.

Such an interpretation sits very uneasily with de Gaulle's determination to strengthen the powers of government, with the internal organisation of the Council and with its early history. Its members are politically appointed and there is no confirmation procedure by a branch of the legislature as happens in the United States. The 1958 Constitution granted exclusive right of access to the Council to the dignitaries of the regime – President of the Republic, Prime Minister, Presidents of the National Assembly and Senate – and did not allow it to be used by individuals or by the court system on appeal. In the early years of the Republic, the Council gained the reputation of being the Executive's creature rather than the Constitution's guardian and of being simply a further way of exorcising the spectre of an over mighty, anti-government legislature. Its refusal to declare unconstitutional de Gaulle's use of Article 11 in the 1962 referendum on the direct election of the presidency came in for particular criticism.

Since 1970, however, the role of the Constitutional Council has grown. In the early 1970s it started to cite the principles of liberty and equality laid down in the preamble to the 1958 Constitution as reasons for striking down measures voted by the governmental majority in the National Assembly. An important constitutional amendment in 1974 allowed access to the Council by any sixty senators and deputies. In 1977 president Giscard d'Estaing asked the Council to decide on the constitutionality of direct elections to the European Parliament. During the 1980s the Council was appealed to extensively by Opposition parliamentarians of both Right and Left and its decisions led to substantial modification of government legislation. Between 1981 and 1986, it overturned part or all of thirty-four laws voted by the Socialist majority in the National Assembly and in the first months of the 1986 Chirac government it gave unqualified approval to only four of the sixteen laws submitted to it. In 1992 the Council declared that ratification of the Maastricht Treaty on European union required an amendment to the Constitution.

The transformation of the Constitutional Council from lap-dog to watchdog is an important development in French politics. It is true that the Council is systematically used as a weapon by both sides in the parliamentary struggle and that appointments to it are made with party considerations in mind. Before the 1986 elections, which the Socialists were certain to lose, President Mitterrand appointed Robert Badinter, one of his closest political allies, as Council president. Gaullist supporters of the Chirac government subsequently denounced a number of its decisions and, in an ironical use of republican discourse by its traditional opponents, spoke of it as a threat to parliamentary sovereignty.

If the United States experience shows that no constitutional court can avoid charges of politicisation, France's Constitutional Council has certainly acquired an authority which it initially lacked. If nothing has so far come of President Mitterrand's suggestion that the Constitution should be amended in order to enable individual citizens to ask the Council to judge on the constitutionality of a law, its role in the system is now assured.

The European Community and the French Constitution

The constitutional status of the European Community raises the same issues of national sovereignty, and identity, in France that it does elsewhere. Thus in 1992 a constitutional amendment was necessary before the Maastricht Treaty could be ratified. The issue of France and the European Community will be dealt with in detail in Chapter 10 but it is worth noting here that the preamble to the 1958 Constitution allows for limitations on sovereignty to organise and protect national security; that Article 55 states that properly ratified international treaties are superior to national laws, so long as they are applied by the other parties; and that France's highest courts have increasingly acknowledged the primacy of Community regulations and directives.

Conclusion

The 1958 Constitution does not enjoy the reverence that has in the past been accorded to its United States equivalent and it is not unknown for politicians and commentators to refer to the possibility of a future Sixth Republic. The reason for this is simple. There have been too many French constitutions for them to become symbols of national identity like 'The Republic' or the Declaration of the Rights and Man and Citizen. Yet the constitutional settlement arrived at between 1958 and 1962, and in particular the direct election of the President, do command widespread acceptance among public opinion and the political parties. A 1992 SOFRES poll, taken at a time of widespread public dissatisfaction with politics, showed that 89 per cent of the French approved of the election of the President by universal suffrage and 61 per cent felt that overall the institutions of the Fifth Republic had worked well. Certainly the system established by de Gaulle has proved flexible enough to survive the many political and social changes France has experienced since 1958. If the test of a constitution's strength is its capacity to survive different balances of political forces, then the text voted in 1958 has been successful. The constitutional bases of French politics look secure.

Further reading

Anne Stevens, *The Government and Politics of France*. London: Macmillan (1992).

Jack Hayward (ed.) *De Gaulle to Mitterrand Presidential Power in France*. London: Hurst (1993).

3
A dual executive?

Constitutions set out the legal framework for the operation of a political system; they do not necessarily tell us very much about who has power. Bagehot's famous distinction between the dignified and the efficient parts of the nineteenth century British Constitution reminds us of this. So too does the obvious fact that 'extra constitutional' powers, be they economic (banks, businesses, trade unions) or political (parties, the press) influence, and may even determine, political outcomes.

In the case of Fifth Republic France, there is another difficulty. Chapter 2 showed that the basic question in any discussion of a political system – who rules? – was not clearly resolved by the 1958 Constitution. The text appears to provide for a parliamentary regime in which the Executive role belongs to prime minister and government. Yet it also gives to the President of the Republic powers greater than that normally attributed to a constitutional head of state; and we have seen that for most of the Fifth Republic the dominant impression has been of a system in which the president determines the composition of government and the content of policy. One way of describing this is to say that the 'heroic leadership' that de Gaulle personified in 1958 has been routinised into what its critics describe as an 'elective dictatorship' or a republican monarchy. Alternatively, one could say that the Executive framework is based on the integration rather than the separation of functions under presidential leadership; as

Anne Stevens says, in the Fifth Republic 'it is impossible to distinguish between "presidential" and "governmental" power' (Stevens 1992, p. 89). A third is to adopt the term 'imperial presidency' that was used to describe United States presidents in the 1960s and 1970s.

Yet the cohabitation periods of 1986–88 and 1993 onwards, when a left-wing president coexisted with a right-wing government, show that the position is actually more complex and that the presidentialist reading of the Fifth Republic is heavily dependent on the existence of mutually supporting majorities in presidency and National Assembly. Cohabitation underlines the point that there is more than one reading of constitutional power in France and that the political composition of the National Assembly will determine whether president or government holds the upper hand.

Hence an understanding of the roles of president and prime minister/government must take account of the political circumstances at any given time. It also needs to recognise that 'leadership' operates along various dimensions. Howard Machin has identified the following areas as together constituting the dimensions of political leadership – symbolic representation, opinion formation, party organisation, ideological production, agenda setting, decision taking and co-ordination (Hall, Hayward, Machin 1990, p. 95). The history of the two presidencies of Mitterrand (1981–88, 1988–) demonstrates that the loss of the leadership role in some areas does not necessarily mean powerlessness in others. Mitterrand's ability to choose, and realise, policy agendas was obviously greater between 1981–86 and 1988–93, when his supporters controlled the National Assembly, than it was between 1986–88 and after March 1993. But he was not reduced in these latter periods to the purely representational role that in the case of Third and Fourth Republic presidents was caricatured as opening chrysanthemum shows.

The difficulty of the task of defining the relationships within the French executive has been compared with that of trying to nail a pudding to a door (Hayward 1993, p. 101). This chapter aims to make sense of the complexity by examining the various types of role that the president plays and then assessing the role of prime minister and government.

The minimalist definition of the Fifth Republic presidency is that of constitutional monarch. As heads of state, presidents represent the legal and political entity called France in its dealings with other such entities – they receive ambassadors and pay official visits to other countries. They also symbolise the unity of the French nation as a community by making official visits across the length of the national territory. The president is titular head of the armed forces, has the judicial power of pardon, is head of the honours system and possesses a number of official residences, of which the most prominent is the Elysée Palace in Paris. This role can be compared with that of a constitutional monarch or a 'non-political' president, as in Italy, Austria, and Germany – or in the Third and Fourth Republics.

There are, however, major differences between 'non-political' heads of state and the Fifth Republic presidency since the latter possesses a number of powers that do not need to be countersigned by any 'responsible' minister. We have seen that Article 5 of the 1958 texts asserts the role of the president as defender of the Constitution and guardian of the continuity of the State, the independence of the national territory, the respect of its treaties and the proper working of its institutions. The term *arbitrage*, used to describe the president's role as 'defender of the constitution', is one that Mitterrand frequently used in the cohabitation periods. Article 16, enabling the president to declare a state of emergency and become a temporary 'legal dictator', ruling by decree, is an extreme example of this guardian function. Others include the right to dissolve the National Assembly and to determine whether a constitutional amendment will be ratified by a parliamentary Congress or a referendum. The president negotiates and ratifies treaties.

Ever since de Gaulle made plain that 'arbitrage' was a synonym for leadership, Fifth Republic presidents have regarded themselves as France's real ruler whenever the political circumstances permit. This view became, as Chapter 2 shows, the key constitutional convention of the Fifth Republic. It means that the president is intimately involved in the areas defined above by Machin and which can be summarised as (a) political management and (b) the formulation of policy. This presidential supremacy is buttressed by the length of the term of office – seven years – and by the absence of constitutional limitations on the right of an incumbent to seek re-election. But we must note once again that these powers, and in particular the second, are heavily dependent on the political relationship existing between president and National Assembly. They have also meant that, in Jack Hayward's words, the Fifth Republic presidency has moved from being the republican sovereign of de Gaulle's ideal (or fantasy) to a partisan statesman (Hayward 1993, p. 20).

We can clarify the thesis of presidential power by looking at its two components:

1. Political management

The most visible ways in which the presidency shapes the overall political environment are in its constitutional right to appoint the prime minister and, on the advice of the latter, the other members of the government. The president chairs the weekly meetings of the Council of Ministers, can summon, or refuse to summon, special sessions of Parliament, and determine their agenda. Thus in Summer 1993 Mitterrand refused to let a special session discuss a proposed change to the status of church schools.

These are powers which exist however weak the president's political position. Between 1986–88 and after March 1993, the president obviously was not free to choose 'his' government or to supervise its work. Nor could he use the right to call a referendum, since this requires a proposal from either National Assembly or government.

When the president has a supportive parliamentary majority, the situation is radically different. There is no tradition of collective cabinet decision-taking in the Fifth Republic; votes are very rarely taken, and the president's decision is final.

The president can summon meetings of individual ministers to decide particular issues and is at the apex of a system of intra-government committees. Members of his personal staff shadow the work of government departments. The General Secretariat of the Presidency acts as the president's eyes and ears in his dealings with government departments. It contains some twenty to thirty officials and is headed by a general secretary, who is the president's closest adviser. The influence of the General Secretary is shown by the fact that many of them (Michel Jobert under Pompidou, Pierre Bérégevoy and Jean Louis Bianco under Mitterrand) have gone on to hold ministerial office. The president also appoints advisers (*conseillers*) to deal with particular areas in which he takes an interest.

He can decide on a change of government to unblock a difficult political situation or to provide a fresh political impetus. Mitterrand did this in 1984, 1991 and in 1992. As we have seen, the presidential power to dismiss governments does not appear in the constitution, but has become part of the constitutional practice of the Fifth Republic. Alternatively the president can indicate support or disapproval for what 'his' governments are doing. This is a particularly useful weapon when his opponents are in office, but it can be used against his own side as well. For example Mitterrand went on television in 1984, without consulting the minister concerned, to announce that he was dropping a major piece of education legislation voted by the Socialist majority in the National Assembly.

With a 'friendly' National Assembly, the president can place supporters in key positions within the apparatus of government. Between 1988 and 1993, Mitterrand's closest political allies held senior government appointments – Pierre Joxe at Interior and Defence, Roland Dumas at the Foreign ministry, Jack Lang at Culture and Education and Pierre Bérégevoy (a long-time Finance minister before being appointed prime minister in 1992). The right of appointment also extends to many important public bodies such as the Constitutional Council, three of whose nine members are appointed by the president. Shortly before

the 1993 elections Pierre Joxe was appointed president of
the Court of Accounts, an influential watchdog over public
expenditure. The power of appointment allows for members of
the president's family and close entourage to be given positions
in public and para-public organisations. It is a convention of
French politics that presidents should be accused of croneyism
in their use of public sector appointments and Mitterrand
has not escaped criticism on this score. Yves Mény, one of
France's leading political scientists, criticised the way in which
one of the president's close friends was nominated to the
Constitutional Council and then to the office of Mediator (the
French ombudsman) while continuing to have an office at the
Elysée Palace (Meny 1992, p. 59).

At all times the president intervenes in the organisation of
party life, despite the fact that the myth of the presidency
places it 'above' politics and that parties are not respected in
France, in the way they have been in the United States, as
the agents of the democratic process (see Chapter 7). No Fifth
Republic president has ever attended a party convention in the
manner of incumbent US presidents. But party management is
an inherent part of the job – a modern president has to create
an electoral coalition that will put him into power and he will
then have to 'nurse' his supporters since he cannot presume
that they will show the unquestioning devotion that de Gaulle
expected (see Chapter 7). President Giscard d'Estaing in 1978
was the guiding force behind the creation of the *Union pour
la Democratie Française*. As president, Mitterrand has kept in
close touch with Socialist leaders and has sought, with varying
success, to influence the composition of its leadership and its
parliamentary representatives. The president can also use his
constitutional prerogatives to destabilise opposition parties. The
1972 referendum which Pompidou held on British entry into
the EEC was designed in part to embarrass the newly formed
alliance between the Socialist and Communist parties. Twenty
years later, the Maastricht referendum called by Mitterrand
aimed to show up the splits within the Right over European
integration.

The president engages in a continuous dialogue with the electorate. The constitutional separation of powers means that, although the president can send messages to Parliament, he may not take part in its proceedings. But television is now the dominant medium through which the president seeks to influence public opinion and all Fifth Republic presidents have made extensive use of it. De Gaulle was a superb manipulator of televised press conferences at which he would set out his views before a spellbound audience of journalists (and members of his own government, who were sometimes observed taking notes). Mitterrand has held fewer full-scale press conferences than any of his predecessors, but he appears frequently on television, sometimes alone and sometimes responding to questions. He also took part in a lengthy television discussion on the Maastricht Treaty shortly before the 1992 referendum during which he debated with Philippe Séguin, a leading Gaullist opponent of the treaty. Since 1974, the most important media event involving the presidency has been the television debate between the two candidates standing on round two of the contest. It is worth noting also that in the first ten years of his presidency, Mitterrand received 2.35 million letters from ordinary citizens (Hayward 1993, p. 70).

2. Policy-making

The extent to which presidents are identified with policy programmes varies. De Gaulle in 1965 simply offered his continuance in office and refused to intervene before round one of the campaign, believing that he would win easily. (He changed his mind when he was forced into a second round run-off). In 1981 Mitterrand, as candidate, presented 110 proposals covering all aspects of national life, whereas seven years later he contented himself with writing a 'letter to all French people' that was long on generalisation and short on policy.

But obviously all presidential elections are fought over rival manifestoes and the leadership function is inseparable from the policy agenda. The crucial distinction is between policy areas over which the president exercises day-to-day control and those which he is prepared to delegate to others.

From the earliest days of the Fifth Republic foreign and defence policy have been regarded as being at the centre of presidential action. That this should be so reflects de Gaulle's determination to restore France's international status and his belief that a successful diplomatic and military policy are the key to a country's well-being. All of de Gaulle's successors have shared this view. It should be noted that the 1958 Constitution, once again, does not contain an unambiguous affirmation of presidential supremacy in the sphere of defence since it makes the prime minister responsible for national defence and for the armed forces. Yet by the mid-1960s it was evident that foreign and defence policy was to be the reserved domain (*domaine réservé*) of the president, a state of affairs symbolised by the 1964 decree entrusting the president with sole responsibility for employing France's independent nuclear deterrent which turned the country, according to one expert, into a nuclear monarchy. Presidents clearly do not make foreign policy on their own – but theirs is the determining voice. The two cohabitation periods have not seriously challenged the presidential authority in foreign and defence policy, although it is significant that shortly before the 1993 parliamentary elections Mitterrand arranged for the establishment of a computerised information service linking his office with the Foreign Office. The fact that this absence of conflict reflects the broad consensus in France over key foreign and defence policy areas (see Chapter 10) suggests that in different circumstances a conflict could arise between President and Government. But so far a, sometimes discordant, harmony has prevailed.

We can see how presidential authority operates by looking in turn at how foreign policy is managed in both crisis and normal circumstances. During the former, the president assumes direct responsibility. This was graphically shown during the Gulf crisis of 1990–91. Mitterrand took personal control of France's diplomatic and military responses to the Iraqi invasion of Kuwait; the prime minister Rocard was sidelined. He was also responsible for explaining French policy to international and national interests. The crisis posed difficult problems of political control, because of the presence in France of numerous Islamic immigrants, the close commercial links between France and Iraq, the Gaullist tradition of hostility to unconditional alignment with the United States and the existence of a strong anti-war party. Mitterrand's handling of the Gulf War showed that the president can derive great prestige from the successful management of international crises. But any political advantage gained may be short lived and Mitterrand's botched response to the attempted Soviet coup in August 1991 indicates the risks involved.

Article 52 of the Constitution lays down that the president negotiates and ratifies treaties with other countries. In normal circumstances the president determines the content of the major themes of foreign policy and the prime minister intervenes in specific areas (e.g. the European Community) only with his acquiescence. It is customary for the foreign minister to be either a close personal associate (as with Mitterrand's long-serving friend Roland Dumas, who held the post between 1984–86 and 1988–93) or a career diplomat with no political profile. Europe has become the corner-stone of French foreign policy (see Chapter 10) and Mitterrand has planned and masterminded French initiatives for economic and political integration. The presidency is also closely involved in France's relations with its former colonies in Africa. Mitterrand attends regular meetings of the Council of the *Francophonie* (a sort of French Commonwealth) and until 1993 his son was the Elysée adviser for African affairs.

Foreign and defence policy are, like the administration of justice, among the functions that define a State – if a political organisation has no authority to enter into treaty agreements with other states, or to assert its will by the use of force, then it cannot be defined as a state. Given that the Constitution makes the president guarantor of the State's continuity, it is inevitable that foreign policy matters loom so large in his profile. This is why any disagreements over foreign policy between president and prime minister would threaten the bases of cohabitation.

Domestic policy

In the early years of the Fifth Republic, the argument put forward by a leading Gaullist politician that foreign and defence policy constituted the 'reserved domain' of the presidency was used to protect de Gaulle from political interference in the formulation of his Algerian policy. It was certainly not regarded by de Gaulle, or by any of his successors, as constituting a restriction on their policy-making powers in any other sphere. French presidents do not necessarily take the initiative in domestic affairs. But when supported by the National Assembly their potential for intervention is great, as the following list demonstrates:

1. Presidents have tastes and their office gives them the power to indulge them. Mitterrand's predecessor, Giscard d'Estaing, slowed down the tempo of the Marseillaise to make it sound less aggressively martial (to his opponents this was a sign of his lack of republican convictions). Mitterrand has become famous as a builder in Paris – the Louvre Pyramid, the Defense Arch, the Bastille Opera and the planned national library.
2. Presidents have policy ambitions and use their control of the political agenda to realise them. Mitterrand has been less interventionist in this respect than his immediate predecessors, who were closely identified with particular areas (Pompidou with industrial policy) or with the whole range of public policy (Giscard sent six-monthly 'agenda setting' letters to his government). Mitterrand, by contrast, left a lot of decision making to his prime ministers and ministers. Yet it would be wrong to underestimate the decisive nature of his interventions, particularly in political emergencies. In 1983 he abandoned the economic policy on

which he had been elected president two years earlier and in 1984 gave up plans for a totally secular school system with which the Socialist Party had been identified since the nineteenth century.

3. Presidents have the power to arbitrate between policy clashes within government. The fact that the prime minister is head of government does not mean that he or she can be assured of having the president's support in ministerial disagreements. Edith Cresson (Prime Minister 1991–92) bitterly complained of the independent policy that her finance minister Bérégevoy was able to pursue with the tacit support of the Elysée.

These three examples show that in 'normal' (i.e. non-cohabitation) circumstances the president largely determines how much autonomy the prime minister and government will have. The latter are not, of course, simple executants of an all-pervasive presidential will. As prime minister between 1988–91, Michel Rocard for example took on the programmes for the introduction of a minimum income provision and the administrative reorganisation of the Paris region. He also attempted to control the explosive dossier of immigration by organising a series of round table meetings of all the political parties. Rocard's short lived successor, Edith Cresson (1991–92) sought to formulate an interventionist industrial policy and Pierre Bérégevoy was strongly identified with the defence of the French franc in the European Monetary System.

But this is devolved, rather than original, authority. It is up to the president to decide what he wants to involve himself with; he is the ultimate court of appeal for disagreements between ministers and between ministers and prime minister. As we have seen, presidents retain the right to distance themselves from the government they appoint, even when it shares their overall political views. At various times Mitterrand criticised what he regarded as government shortcomings. For example in 1990–91 he received delegations of striking high school students and of immigration associations. And he allowed his lack of sympathy with the personality and methods of his prime minister Rocard to be generally known.

The role of prime minister and government

John Nance Garner, who was Franklin Roosevelt's vice president between 1933–40, famously described the office he held as not being worth a pitcher of warm spit. It is a description that has sometimes seemed appropriate to the prime ministers of the Fifth Republic. On the surface, the presidentialising of politics in the Fifth Republic has transformed the prime minister from head of government to presidential agent. It is true that the chronic ministerial instability of the assembly-dominated Third and Fourth Republics meant that the authority of prime ministers before 1958 was, to say the least, insecure. But their title – President of the Council of Ministers – underlined their formal pre-eminence within government.

Things look very different in the Fifth Republic. Anne Stevens (1992, p. 95) notes that de Gaulle disliked the use of the term 'chef de gouvernement' (head of government) to designate the prime minister. The latter is chosen by the president and in 'normal' circumstances derives his political legitimacy from the president. We have seen that a prime minister's tenure in office depends on presidential goodwill; in 1991 Mitterrand dismissed his prime minister Rocard virtually on the spot.

The fact that only three of the fourteen prime ministers of the Fifth Republic have been appointed immediately after a legislative election demonstrates the 'presidential' source of their authority. Two of these three cases – Chirac (1986) and Balladur (1993) – reflected the defeat of the president's party in legislative elections. The third occurred in 1968 when de Gaulle appointed a new prime minister, Couve de Murville, precisely because the existing one, Pompidou, was so popular. Newly-appointed prime ministers do not necessarily seek a vote of confidence from the National Assembly to whom they are responsible and the composition of their government normally depends on the approval of the president. The years 1986 and 1993 obviously mark an exception to this. Cohabitation is the only time when regular meetings of the Cabinet, presided over by the prime minister, occur alongside the Council of Ministers, which the president chairs.

Yet the president's constitutional right to hire, and his – unconstitutional – power to fire, do not mean that the Fifth Republic prime ministers, and their ministerial colleagues, have become mere agents of the presidential will. Fifth Republic governments have contained between twenty-six and forty-eight ministers, the most important of whom run massive departments like Finances, Education, the Interior, Defence and Health. The current (1993) government of Balladur has twenty-nine members of various degrees of seniority. Every minister has a sizeable private office (*cabinet*) to enable her or him to liaise with the permanent administration of the department and with other government departments.

To understand the role of prime minister and government in the Fifth Republic it is clearly necessary to distinguish between the periods when their authority derives from the president and those when it rests on the support of the National Assembly. In the latter, prime minister and government do indeed 'determine the policy of the Nation'; in the former their role is to govern, but not necessarily to choose. But even in 'normal' circumstances, the prime minister is one of the key actors in the political system, performing a role without which it cannot operate. Raymond Barre, a former prime minister, wrote in 1987 that 'the President of the Republic can do nothing without the Hotel Matignon (the prime minister's residence). The prime minister orchestrates the music composed by the President'. If one or two prime ministers (Couve de Murville 1968–69, Pierre Messmer 1972–74) are regarded as having been little more than pliant chiefs of staff, many others have been substantial figures, with considerable influence over the formulation of policy, the administration of government and the management of politics.

French politics today

We have noted that prime ministers can provide the impetus for particular policy initiatives – so long as the president is content for them to do so. They also have the responsibility for resolving, or at least coping with, domestic issues – public sector strikes, agricultural disturbances and so on. All of them are closely involved in the preparation of the annual budget and in resolving spending disputes between government departments and the Finance Ministry; on occasion (i.e. Barre (1976–81), Bérégevoy (1992–93)) they have taken overall responsibility for economic policy. More generally they are responsible for preserving governmental cohesion in a system that lacks the British expectation of collective ministerial solidarity. They have an extensive private office (*cabinet*) to enable them to dominate the extensive network of interministerial committees that exists to co-ordinate action. (With twenty-five members, Balladur's 1993 *cabinet* was one of the smallest in recent years.) The director of the prime minister's cabinet is recognised as her or his spokesperson in dealing with other ministers – and with the Elysée staff.

The prime minister has important administrative and co-ordination functions. The French presidency does not have anything resembling a United States-style Executive Office, and the prime minister runs the equivalent to the British Cabinet office. The key administrative service he or she controls is the General Secretariat, the body responsible for organising, administering, co-ordinating and recording government decisions. The prime minister determines the specific competences of the individual ministers. He or she also has the right to nominate three members of the Constitutional Council and shares with the president the right to nominate to posts within the civil service and public sector. The power of patronage may be shared with the President; but its value to a prime minister in building up a network of grateful supporters is real enough.

Chapter 2 showed that the prime minister is the indispensable link between the two sources of political authority in the Fifth Republic – presidency and National Assembly. Appointed by the one, s/he is politically responsible to the other. Given the constitutional irresponsibility of president to National Assembly, it is the prime minister's task to ensure that policy becomes law and to defend the government's actions to the legislature. Government bills are prepared and then navigated through both houses of Parliament by prime minister and team, including a minister whose special task is relations with Parliament. The experience of the Rocard government of 1988–91 showed that this can be a very time-consuming business. Government actions, and inactions, also have to be explained and justified by the prime minister to parliament and the media.

The tasks of political management do not stop there. One of de Gaulle's ambitions in the early Fifth Republic was to 'depoliticise' power by separating government from the parties. To this end he appointed a number of senior ministers from outside Parliament and introduced the constitutional prohibition on ministers from being members of parliament. The idea that government could be inoculated from the virus of party politics is, however, inherently impossible in a parliamentary system based on parties. While it is true that in recent years as many as 30 per cent of government ministers have not been parliamentarians when appointed to office, the party-based nature of government is obvious. And to the extent that all French governments contain representatives from more than one party, one of the prime minister's most important tasks is keeping the coalition together. The task is particularly difficult when the prime minister is not the leader of the majority group in the government coalition. As prime minister, Raymond Barre faced great difficulties with the neo-Gaullist RPR (Rassemblement pour la République) in the late 1970s. A new dimension to this prime ministerial task emerged in 1993 with the appointment of Balladur. Balladur is not the leader of the dominant party in the parliamentary majority and will have to negotiate with its president Chirac as well as with other parties represented in his government.

Conclusion

Our survey of the structures and practices that shape governmental power in France reveals three dominant characteristics:

1. So long as the National Assembly backs the president,
   there is neither a dyarchy at the summit of the Fifth
   Republic nor a United States-style 'double presidency',
   strong in foreign affairs but weak in domestic affairs. But
   presidential government does not usually mean government
   by the president. With the support of the president and the
   backing of the National Assembly, the government does
   indeed shape the content of domestic policy – 94 per cent
   of all laws in 1989 originated in government bills – and
   the prime minister does control her or his government.
   President and prime minister do not need to enjoy close
   personal relations for the system to work – Mitterrand got
   on so badly with Rocard that some commentators spoke of
   his premiership as a new cohabitation – but each accepts
   the conventions that have emerged since 1958.
2. The presidency operates within an overall political environment which necessarily affects its autonomy, even when it is
   not faced, as in 1986 and 1993, with a hostile majority in
   the National Assembly. The composition of the government
   has to be chosen to take account of current political realities
   inside and outside the National Assembly. In April 1992
   Mitterrand was forced against his will to replace his prime
   minister (and protégée) Cresson because her unpopularity
   had become so great that the Socialist leadership in the
   National Assembly threatened to rebel.
3. There are other constraints, formal and informal, on the
   freedom of presidential and governmental action. Impeach-
   ment by Parliament is an extreme example of the former,
   another is the power of the Constitutional Council to
   strike down a measure which the president supports, and
   which has been passed by the National Assembly. The
   National Assembly has the power to defeat a government

by passing a vote of censure. More fundamentally, the capacity of the French president and his agents to set out and implement a policy agenda is as vulnerable as its equivalents elsewhere to the pressures that have resulted from the internationalising of economic activity. The Fifth Republic has been successful in asserting the authority of presidency and government, whatever the balance of power between them may be. But in today's 'global village' there are pressures that even this authority cannot defy.

Further reading

Jack Hayward, *De Gaulle to Mitterrand: Presidential Power in France.* London: Hurst (1993).

Vincent Wright, *The Government and Politics of France* London: Unwin Hyman (1989).

4
Government and 'The State'

In France as elsewhere, modern government is big government. Over five million people, 30 per cent of the working population, are employed by one or other branches of the public sector and 44 per cent of national income goes in taxation. To the 'traditional' functions of government – defence, law and order, diplomacy – have been added the newer tasks of economic management and welfare provision. The spending ministries have budgets that run into many billions of pounds and the biggest of them all, Education, employs over a million officials.

But if French government resembles that of other industrialised states, many observers claim that the way in which it is organised, the functions it fulfills and the style of its interventions are exceptional. Three points in particular are highlighted:

1. The French economy remains the most State-dominated in the Group of Seven capitalist industrialised nations.
2. In comparison with other European countries, France is an 'administrative State' in which central government controls, or at least supervises, activities that elsewhere are left to independent organisations.
3. Senior public officials exercise strong influence over policy-making and form an elite that dominates the commanding heights of the political economy and even, according to some observers, constitutes France's 'governing class'.

The purpose of this chapter is to examine some of the claims that are made about the French State and to describe the principal areas of its activity.

The myth of the French State and its critics

Chapter 1 noted that the idea of the State, and the term itself, are ubiquitous in French politics in a way that they are not in Britain or the United States, where the term government is more commonly used. The belief that France – a large country whose 'natural' frontiers are not always clearly defined – owes its existence to the State is one that pre-dates the Revolution and was greatly reinforced by it. That is why historical figures like Louis XIV's minister Jean Baptiste Colbert, the Jacobins and Bonaparte are so frequently cited in analyses of French government. The concept of nationalisation itself dates from the Revolution.

To a British or American observer, what gives the concept of the State in France its specificity are the autonomy it possesses *vis-à-vis* other institutions, and notably the courts; its selfconscious role as guardian of the public interest; and the centralised and uniform way in which the administration is organised. The State is portrayed as a distinct entity, with clear rights and duties, and possessing its own rules of procedure that are independent of the ordinary law. The French system of administrative law, headed by the Conseil d'Etat, means that the Administration is judge of its own actions and cannot be sued in the ordinary courts. The State also enjoys an important symbolic role as the incarnation of a General Interest, which is separate from – and superior to – the plural interests of private groups. It thus becomes a player rather than a referee, empowered to give a lead to social groups rather than simply to mediate between their aims. The American political scientist Wiliam Safran speaks of 'autonomous governmental preferences' that claim to provide a rational definition of the public interest.

According to the statist model, public officials have the authority that derives from their identification with State goals. Defined as functionaries (*fonctionnaires*) rather than as civil servants, the most senior of them, who belong to the so-called *grands corps* (see below) are regarded by their admirers as possessing a more disinterested approach to the public good, and greater functional competence, than party politicians. To their critics, as we shall see, they form an undemocratic governing elite.

One example of the perceived salience of the State is its relationship to the post-war French economy. Assessments of Britain's relatively poor post-war economic performance often point to the important role of the French State in encouraging and managing the process of modernisation that turned a society of farmers and small businessmen into one of Europe's most successfully industrialised economies. Confidence in the virtues of statist interventionism was not, as in Britain or the United States, restricted to parties of the Left; General de Gaulle and many of his followers were convinced of the government's ability – and right – to plan the economy and to channel public resources in the right direction.

There is, of course, another side to the story. Critics of the French State have always complained about its excessive pretensions – its mania for regulating society and interfering in the nooks and crannies of everyday life. They point to the thousands of laws, decrees and regulations that pour out of government departments – 125,516 between 1971–81 – and claim that it is no accident that the word bureaucracy is French in origin. The State and its officials are also accused of authoritarianism and lack of accountability, for example in the way in which State officials simply declare their actions to be in the 'general interest' and hence absolved from scrutiny or challenge. The Fifth Republic, like its predecessors, is littered with examples of unsanctioned bureaucratic scandals. Other critics, from the great nineteenth-century liberal Alexis de Tocqueville onwards, have pointed to the role of the State and its officials in stifling the emergence of a democratic civic culture in which ordinary citizens are able to run their own affairs. The frequency with which protesting groups resort to violence to achieve their aims can also be explained by the State's refusal to acknowledge the legitimacy of pressure groups (see Chapter 9).

A different, and on the surface contradictory, critique emphasises the inefficiency, and lack of internal coherence, that characterise the various branches of the government machine and make it impossible to talk about 'the State' as if it were a homogeneous, rational machine. Denunciations of the slowness and lack of co-ordination of government departments are a staple part of French public debate and administrative analysis. Experienced analysts of the French administration like Wright (1989) and Stevens (1992) point to the rivalries and inconsistencies that exist at all levels of the administration, making a mockery of its claims to rationality, and to the ability of well-organised groups within society to coerce this supposedly 'rational' powerhouse. We shall see that in recent years there has been in France, as elsewhere, a decline in confidence in the economic merits of public ownership and in the need for central control over local government (see Chapter 6).

The idea that senior public officials form a community of public-spirited guardians free from political influence can also be attacked. Political intervention in the management of the bureaucracy has always been much greater than the myth of the impartial State would suggest. In the case of some four hundred top positions, the government of the day can appoint whoever it wants and this certainly allows for the extensive exercise of patronage by the politically powerful.

Clearly, the thrust of these criticisms varies. Some depend upon judgements about what government *ought* to be like in a free society, others on an assessment of the organisational *efficiency* of French government. Moreover the problem with all such overarching analyses of 'the State' is that they do not distinguish sufficiently between its various elements: dynamic interventionism of some sectors is matched by the obsessive routinism with which others can paralyse individual, and group, initiatives. We shall see below that the mystique of the State and the belief in the virtues of interventionism are less evident now than they were in the early post-war decades when powerful forces on the Right (de Gaulle) and Left (Communists and Socialists) believed in statist solutions to societal problems. That this should be so reflects the growing internationalisation of the French economy as well as the global ideologial disillusionment with the effectiveness of state interventionism. Yet state expectations remain high in France and the following section will show just how extensive the area of governmental interventions remains.

What government does

1. Law and order

Two basic tasks of government are to defend its citizens from outsiders and from each other. The Ministries of Defence and of Foreign Affairs are between them responsible for maintaining France's security and diplomatic interests. To the extent that the latter are increasingly concentrated on the European Community, they will be dealt with in Chapter 10. France also has extensive, strategically important territories overseas (notably in the South Pacific) and continues to have an independent nuclear deterrent. The Ministry of Defence has an annual budget (1991) of 200 billion francs. It is responsible for administering France's programme of compulsory, male military service and for a 250,000-strong professional army. It also promotes France's huge armaments industry.

Law enforcement and the administration of justice are, together with the organisation of national defence, among the defining functions of states ancient and modern. In the Fifth Republic, the President of the Republic is entrusted with the protection of the independence of the judiciary and he presides over the High Council of the Magistrature. The administration of the courts is in the hands of the Minister of Justice (*Garde des sceaux*) who is responsible for the appointment, training and career structure of magistrates; for penal policy; and for the overall administration of the legal professions. Since the administration of justice is a public service, French theory and tradition require that it be administered by public officials. There is no real parallel in France for the British system of lay Justices of the Peace or for the United States practice of electing county lower-court judges. The role of the jury is also more circumscribed.

In 1991 the then prime minister Michel Rocard declared that the administration of justice was the priority concern of government; a year later a public opinion poll showed that 82 per cent of the French believed that judges were subject to political influence. Such facts reflect the widely held belief in France that the administration of the judicial system, and justice itself, are in crisis. It is not unknown for magistrates to demonstrate in the street against government policy.

Part of the reason for this is financial. The budget of the Justice Ministry in 1991 was 1.42 per cent of total government expenditure, an increase over the last ten years but still barely more than that of the ministry of Culture. The Justice Ministry is responsible for the administration of the prison system, where rising expenditure has failed to solve the problems of overcrowding and consequent unrest. France's 6000 professional judges, who are trained at a National School for Magistrates, are not particularly well paid and do not enjoy high social status. The French constitutional expert Olivier Duhamel cites as evidence of the low political status of the Justice Ministry the fact that in 1990 a simple demonstration by sixth formers led to the budget of the Education Ministry being given extra credits equivalent to 30 per cent of Justice's budget (Duhamel 1991, p. 59).

But the real problem is one of confidence rather than finance, and derives from the belief that the courts do not constitute a genuinely independent 'third power'. That the constitution does not acknowledge the existence of a 'judicial power' but merely of a 'judicial authority' reflects the deep-rooted suspicion, dating from the Revolution, of the threat posed to democracy by a 'government of judges'. But it is also argued that the courts are susceptible to political pressure from government. This is explained in terms of the alleged ability of the Justice Minister (inevitably a political appointee) to influence the outcome of sensitive cases by his control of procedures. A celebrated example occurred in 1987 when a magistrate allowed a suspected Iranian terrorist to leave the country after the most perfunctory interrogation. Magistrates are divided into two categories – those who hear cases and those who are members of the Parquet and act as public prosecutors. The former have security of tenure, the latter are under the control of the Justice Ministry which can decide to bury an embarrassing case or paralyse the attempts of examining magistrates to investigate it. Magistrates' careers are determined by a High Council of the Magistrature. From 1958 until the Constitutional amendment of 1993 all the Council's members were appointed by the President of the Republic.

That court decisions are frequently publicly challenged by politicians and others reflects the aggressive style of French political debate, and the legacy of France's troubled past. (It is significant that modern France's most famous political crisis, the Dreyfus Affair, began as a miscarriage of justice.) In 1992 the decision of a court not to proceed with a case against a notorious official of the Vichy police (the *affaire Touvier*) provoked a storm of protest. Yet the controversy surrounding the administration of justice also reflects the determination of some magistrates to pursue potentially embarrassing cases and the media interest that this arouses. In 1992 an examining magistrate undertook highly publicised investigations of the financial affairs of the governing Socialist Party; details of his intention to prosecute senior party members (including the president of the National Assembly) appeared in the press before the recipients were informed. In Summer 1992 France's most senior judge, the president of the Appeal Court (Cour de Cassation), wrote formally to the Justice Minister to express his concern at the prevailing tone of public debate about judicial independence.

The experience of the British judicial system in Northern Ireland (and elsewhere) demonstrates the difficulties in combining considerations of security with the imperatives of justice. Thus the experience of France is not unique. The difference is that France has not, and does not, regard its justice system with the veneration – some would say the complacency – that has existed in the English-speaking democracies and that there is no entrenched culture of the independence of judges (Mény 1991, p. 142). It should be noted, however, that since 1982 French citizens have been allowed to appeal to the European Commission on Human Rights against decisions of the judiciary and police (Hall, Hayward, Machin 1990, p. 228). A 1993 law has sought to strengthen the legal rights of suspects held on remand.

France has over 200,000 police officers, a higher percentage per head of population than in Britain, Germany and Spain. The bulk of its police forces are under the control of the Interior Ministry although the 88,000 gendarmes, which service rural areas and have public order responsibilities, come under the Ministry of Defence. Some local authorities also run a municipal police force. Relations between the different police forces are often extremely bad.

One of the major charges against police is the authoritarianism and on occasion brutality with which they carry out their public order functions, and the absence of redress available to innocent citizens they mistreat. This was particularly, but not exclusively, true of the politically charged early years of the Fifth Republic. In 1961 some two hundred Algerian demonstrators were killed by police action in Paris and the riot police (Compagnies républicaines de la sécurité) acquired a worldwide notoriety for the way in which the student demonstrations of 1968 were repressed. Procedures for obtaining redress of grievance against police misdemeanours are weak. France's intelligence services have also had their share of scandals. The most notorious in recent years was the *Rainbow Warrior* Affair (1985) in which agents of the secret services blew up a boat owned by the environmental group Greenpeace and killed one of its members. Attempts by Parliament to control the activities of the intelligence services have been unsuccessful.

It is important to remember, once again, that France does not have a monopoly of complaints against the police forces. The difference is that the French have never thought that their policemen are wonderful.

2. 'Hearts and minds'

All modern states take a keen interest in the education and training of their citizens. Anxieties about the economic consequences of an ill- or inappropriately-educated youth loom large on the policy agendas of Britain and the United States as well as France. There is, however, more to education than the acquisition of practical, or intellectual, skills. The training (*formation*) that school provides also seeks to socialise the future citizens of a country in such a way that a consensus exists around certain shared cultural and political values.

The close involvement of the French State in education will be no surprise to anyone familiar with France's history. The 1789 revolutionaries believed that knowledge was the way in which individuals could realise the potentialities that were inherent in human reason; the Jacobin leader Danton once said that the People's prime need, after bread, was education. There was also a more political reason for the State to concern itself with national education. With the breakdown of the 1789 consensus and the emergence of the conflict between the clerical Right and the secular Republic, the two forces battled for control of the hearts and minds of the Nation.

One of the principal aims of the Third Republic (1875–1940) was to ensure that a public system of education existed in which future citizens would learn the virtues of civic patriotism and would be shielded from the anti-republican teaching of the Church. To this day, state schools are not allowed to teach religious knowledge or to hold assemblies at which prayers are said. The system placed control of teaching and teachers in the hands of the Paris-based Ministry of Education and its territorial officials, the *recteurs d'académie*. Local authorities had virtually no say in the organisation of schooling and although church schools did exist (they are called *écoles libres*) they did not receive any public money and the religious orders that ran them were periodically banned. As John Ambler says '. . . particularly since the Third Republic, Paris has prescribed curriculum, hired teachers, allocated funds and in general presided over an educational system that is more centralized than those found in other Western democracies' (Hollifield and Ross 1991, p. 195). The school education of 13 million students is controlled directly or indirectly by a Ministry of Education that employs over a million officials, 770,000 as teachers. The education budget for 1991 was 263 billion francs – a fifth of total government expenditure – and to this should be added the 48 billion francs spent on education and training by other ministries and the 48 billion francs raised by local authorities.

Higher, as well as elementary and secondary education, is closely supervised, and financed, by central government. One and a half million students are enrolled in some form of post-secondary education. Universities are not allowed to award their own degrees, or to appoint their own permanent staff without approval from a national committee appointed by the Ministry. The State also runs a large number of training schools for its own future officials, some of which date back to the eighteenth and nineteenth centuries. The most famous of them are known as the *grandes écoles* (Ecole Polytechnique, Ecole des Mines, Ecole des Ponts et Chaussées, Ecole Normale Supérieure, Ecole Nationale d'Administration). They enjoy immense prestige and their alumni can expect to acquire top positions in the public, and private, sectors (see below).

Although the organisation of education in France provides a good example of the scale of State interventionism, it also shows that government can become the victim of its own responsibilities. Educational problems provided the Fifth Republic with the biggest challenge to its authority to date, in the student riots of 1968. The basic reason for the riots was the inefficiency and authoritarianism with which the expansion of the university sector had been managed. Twenty-five years later, in spite of attempts at reform, the education system remains a controversial subject. In the 1980s mass protest led to the abandonment of reform projects by governments both of the Left (the Savary law, 1984) and Right (the Devaquet bill of 1986). More recently, the appointment of Jack Lang as Education Minister in 1992 was followed by the partial withdrawal of the secondary school proposals of his predecessor. The power of pressure groups in education is considerable. It shows that state supervision can result in responsibility without power.

The State does not limit its interest in education to schooling; it also has a role to play in the organisation of the media and in the propagation of culture. In both areas important, albeit contrasting, changes have occurred. The government provides greater financial backing to the newspaper press than that available in other countries, in the form of advantageous postal and fiscal arrangements, in order to ensure pluralism of opinion. More than 50 per cent of the income of France's leading news agency, Agence France Presse, derives from subscriptions from government bodies. The 1980s saw a relaxation in the traditionally tight control that French governments have exercised over broadcasting. Governments both of the Left and the Right have contributed to the deregulation. The Left liberalised the radio airwaves and allowed the creation of a subscription-based television station Canal Plus and two other private channels. The Right privatised TF1, hitherto the largest public sector television station. (Mitterrand blamed the electoral rout of the Socialists in 1993 on the anti-government stance of TF1.) The reorganisation of the audiovisual media, and the controversies surrounding the succession of regulatory bodies that have been established to control them, demonstrate government's interest in the media landscape. France no longer has a Minister of Information but the prime minister's office runs a large information office, the *Service d'information et de documentation*.

Culture is not a word of which the French are afraid. The promotion of French culture, and of the French language, has been a concern of governments in the Fifth Republic ever since de Gaulle made the distinguished writer André Malraux Minister of Cultural Affairs in 1959. In the 1980s, the resources and profile of the Ministry of Culture have risen. Its share of the State budget has risen from 0.46 per cent in 1980 to 0.94 per cent in 1991. In his study of the evolution of the French State since 1789, Pierre Rosanvallon points out that culture, like finance and diplomacy, is seen as part of its *raison d'être* rather than as something in which it merely takes an interest (Rosanvallon 1990, p. 110). Very few Anglo-Saxon countries have a ministry of culture of the French type, although the Heritage Department created by Britain's Conservative government after the 1992 election was inspired by it. France's film industry receives extensive government subsidies.

Another sign of the State's desire to promote national culture is its concern to protect the French language from being corrupted by Americanisms and to promote its use abroad. The almost caricatural sensitivity of government to issues of the national language was shown by the decision of the Rocard government in June 1989 to establish a High Council for French Spelling which was entrusted with deciding, *inter alia*, how hyphens should be used.

3. Welfare

With France's social security system, we move into an area that both reinforces and challenges the conventional image of a statist system. On the one hand the French have a strong attachment to a comprehensive, publicly funded welfare state, (*Etat providence*). Consolidated, as elsewhere in Europe, after the Second World War, the welfare state provides high standards of health care, retirement pensions and a range of social payments, the most generous of which are family allowances. The system is extremely expensive to run but there is absolutely no evidence that public opinion favours a reduction in its scope. The American observer Douglas Ashford observes that even before the Socialists came to power in 1981 'France had a system of social benefits and social programs that equalled that of any of the major European states, and that in spending terms was in advance of Britain, Italy and Germany' (Hollifield and Ross 1991, p. 164). For all the interest shown by French conservatives in American theories of public choice, the right-wing government of 1986–88 did not engage in the anti-statist welfare policies of its British and American equivalents, though it did restore the private hospital beds that Jack Ralite, communist minister of health between 1981 and 1984, had abolished.

It is the organisation of the social security system that breaks with the pattern of statism and universalism. Social security is organised through a network of agencies which employ their own staff and are decentralised and autonomous and increasingly organised through local government. Since 1945, the various funds (*caisses*) – illness, unemployment, retirement – have been administered by contributors, employees and employers and the social security budget is distinct from the national one. The ministries of labour and social services between them take only 10.5 per cent of the total state budget and their political status is low (Hall, Hayward, Machin 1990, p. 191). French health policy also adheres to the principles of liberal medicine, which means that patients are not registered with one doctor but go wherever they like and reclaim the money from the fund. Given that doctors enjoy freedom of prescription, there is no control of expenditure on medicine and the French consume more pills than any other European Community country.

As elsewhere, the problems of social welfare focus on its spiralling costs. Whereas tax levels have tended to stabilise in recent years, social security charges are constantly rising and the health service budget is in massive deficit. The whole system is characterised by a 'structured pluralism' in which the producers and clients call the shots and governments find it very difficult to reduce overall costs.

4. *The economy*

In comparison with English-speaking countries, the French State has a long tradition of intervention in the economy;

laissez-faire is not a practice which has been much practised in the country that coined the term. Forms of interventionism have, of course, varied over time. Before the Second World War, governments concentrated on building tariff walls to protect a small-scale agriculture and industry from the rigours of overseas competition. The trauma of defeat in 1940 led to a demand for industrial modernisation that many politicians and economists felt could only come from the State. The nationalisations of 1945–46 included banks and insurance companies as well as major utilities and the Renault car company, and were complemented by the introduction of economic forecasting and accounting agencies and the creation of a National Planning Commissariat charged with drawing up four-year plans for development. De Gaulle, who never had much respect for the profit motive (or for the patriotism of French businessmen), was a strong believer in the virtues of the Plan.

Post-war France was not a command economy like the socialist states of eastern Europe, and in the 1960s the profit motive was accepted as the motor of industrial growth. Yet even under the presidencies of such champions of capitalism as Pompidou and Giscard d'Estaing, the State continued to play an important role in shaping the economy. The government controlled the supply of credit; it continued to fix many prices; it intervened forcibly to promote industrial reorganisation and mergers (Rosanvallon 1990, p. 260). It also promoted regional development through the *Délégation à l'administration du territoire et à l'action régionale*. The aim was less the encouragement of domestic competition than the creation of 'national champions' capable of resisting the power of the multinationals. The scale of State investment can be seen by the speed with which France completed a massive nuclear energy programme in the 1970s, modernised its telecommunications systems and developed the high speed train (TGV – Train de Grande Vitesse) network. Once the recession struck in 1974, the government laid down tough controls on employers' rights to make workers redundant.

The 1980s saw markedly contrasting governmental attitudes towards interventionism, the end result of which has been to reduce – but by no means to abolish – the State's role in the French economy. The Left came to power in 1981 committed to what Alain Lipietz calls 'national developmentalism'. This took two forms. One was the use of Keynesian techniques of pump-priming to stimulate demand – wages and social payments went up and new civil servants were hired. The other was the pursuit of economic and industrial restructuring via a massive programme of nationalisation. Forty-nine companies and banks were taken into public ownership and annual aid to French industry rose from 35 billion francs in 1981 to 86 billion francs in 1985 (Hall, Hayward, Machin 1990, p. 177).

Two years later the Socialist government embarked on a radical policy shift, which involved acceptance of the international (or at least European) market economy and of the price mechanism and a commitment to a stable currency. Government subsidies to nationalised industries were reduced, as was the regulatory framework covering what public sector companies could and could not do. Corporate profitability was encouraged through restrictions on pay and reductions in company taxation and the government took measures to encourage the growth of the private capital markets.

This was not so much a U-turn as a new start. The right-wing government of Jacques Chirac (1986–88) went further along the new road by privatising many of the companies nationalised in, and before, 1981. For the first time in modern France, the 'anglo-saxon' dogmas of market forces and economic liberalism were openly preached by parties of government. It is noteworthy that the Socialist governments of 1988–93 did not reverse the new approach. Prime minister Rocard emphasised the virtues of balanced budgets and company profitability; his industry minister Roger Fauroux was committed to the encouragement of overseas investment in France and to a reduction in public investment in declining industries; and Bérégevoy, the finance minister, embarked on a further programme of partial privatisations, despite Mitterrand's 1988 campaign pledge that no more would be undertaken. The attempts of Madame Cresson to return to a more activist industrial policy to combat rising unemployment were unsuccessful and her aggressive language towards the Stock Exchange provoked much criticism. The 1993 Balladur government immediately introduced legislation to sell off twenty-one publicly-owned companies and announced plans to give the Bank of France independence from central government.

That the earlier consensus among elites about the virtues of economic interventionism has been partly replaced by a belief in markets and entrepreneurs represents a significant shift in attitudes to the capacity of the State. But the public sector remains very strong in France. More than twenty-four of its largest corporations – from aerospace to Renault, railways to electricity generation (and distribution), to banks and insurance companies – are still (1993) publicly owned. The privatisation policy of the Chirac government was highly illiberal in the way in which the Finance Ministry decided who would control the newly privatised companies. The 1993 Balladur proposals did not include the big monopoly utilities like electricity and railways. Mitterrand has signalled his hostility to the privatisation of key strategic industries like aeronautics, air transport and oil.

An administrator's State: public servants or power elite?

The alleged power of the higher ranks of the Administration has been a constant theme in analyses of the political system of the Fifth Republic. It is argued that *la haute fonction publique* does not simply exercise great influence *within* the governmental machine (as its Whitehall equivalent is said to do) but has been increasingly able to colonise the 'commanding heights' within France's political economy.

The influence that top public officials wield is explained not simply by the interventionist style of French government described above but also by the way in which they are recruited, trained and employed. France's administrative elite is recruited from one of a number of specialist schools (the *grandes écoles*) and then assigned to one of a number of elite agencies known as the *grands corps*. Access to the *grandes écoles* is via a rigorous, and highly competitive, examination system. The Ecole Nationale d'Administration (ENA), founded in 1945, is the legendary recruiting ground for membership of the non-technical corps (the Council of State, the Court of Accounts and the Finance Inspectorate). The technical *grands corps* (Mining, Bridges and Highway Engineers) recruit from the equally prestigious Ecole Polytechnique.

The myth of the 'administrators' State' derives from three factors. In the first place, membership of a *grand corps*, and training at a *grande école*, confers great prestige on the very small numbers who are brainy enough to obtain them. The ruthlessness of the recruitment procedure – only a handful are invited to join each of the *grands corps* every year – confers a halo of excellence on those who successfully navigate it. In the case of the *corps*, small is powerful. Secondly, members of the *grands corps* obtain the plum positions within the Administration, not only in the sphere for which they are formally responsible but right across the board, including the private offices (*cabinets*) of ministers. The *grands corps* control their own career structures and colonise particular divisions within governmental departments. Thirdly, a period in the service of the State is regarded as a springboard into top positions right across the board. The 450 members of the technical Mining Corps fill the boardrooms of France's largest companies. Many of France's leading politicians of both Right and Left (Giscard d'Estaing, Chirac, Rocard, Fabius, Seguin, Juppé) have been through the Ecole Nationale d'Administration and the non-technical grands corps.

Two words – *énarchie* and *pantouflage* – entered general usage in the 1960s as descriptions of the system in which an interlocking elite dominates all categories of decision-taking centres in France. The former refers to the pervasive influence of the graduates of the Ecole Nationale d'Administration and the latter to the practice whereby members of the higher administration swap their jobs for senior positions in the private sector. In 1984 a group of ENA graduates took out an advertisement in France's leading newspaper *Le Monde* offering their talents to the private sector. A 1991 enquiry showed that in a three-month period, 40 per cent of all promotions and appointments in public/private sector companies went to former members of the higher administration. (Mény 1992, p. 119). Government proposals in 1991 to shift the Ecole Nationale d'Administration from Paris to Strasbourg were greeted with outrage by students, staff and alumni who regarded the move as a calculated assault on their status as the State's officer class.

The idea that France is ruled by its officials is, like all such mono-causal explanations, an exaggeration. The claim that the system of *grandes écoles* and *grands corps* produces a unified technocratic elite does not accord easily with the wide diversity of political parties which many civil servants join, or with the tendency of incoming governments to make sweeping personnel changes in sensitive administrative posts. We should note also that a career in public service is no longer the favoured choice of the ambitious young; if it were, then presumably not so many of them would leave the civil service for politics or the private sector. In recent years the numbers applying to the Ecole Nationale d'Administration have stagnated while business school diplomas are ever more popular.

What is true is that State-trained elites dominate the decision-taking centres of present-day France. Membership of a *grand corps* is regarded as the best passport to top positions in both public and private sectors and the very success of the *pantouflage* system ensures, paradoxically, that the Administration continues to attract the brightest students. The possibility for a *grand corps* member who has gone into politics to return to his corps is seen as promoting the diffusion of talent across the system. The power of the administrative–political–industrial complex is all the greater in that its sustaining myth is professional excellence (exams) rather than social acceptability (the old school tie). Critics argue that there is virtually no restriction on senior officials going to work for companies with which their ministries have close dealings. Defenders of the system reply that in a free society talented people can serve the public interest just as well in industry as in government and that the network of bureaucrats, bankers and businessmen is an important reason for France's economic successes.

Conclusion

The French writer Jacques Chevalier has spoken of the decline in the 'myth of the State' that has occurred in France. The State has lost its reputation for omniscience and the development of the *'Etat de droit'* – in which individual rights are not viewed as secondary to a mythical 'general interest' – attacks the theory of the State as voice of the Nation. The growth of independent administrative authorities, of local government autonomy and of the powers of the European Community necessarily weaken the hegemonic pretensions of government and its officials.

The French State is not, however, about to wither away. As prime minister, Michal Rocard referred to the importance of rendering the State not smaller but better (*mieux d'Etat*). This chapter has shown the inadequacy of the thesis of the State as leviathan; but it has also demonstrated the extent to which France remains what it was in the heyday of de Gaulle's Republic – 'a much-governed society'.

Further reading

James F. Hollifield and George Ross (eds), *Searching for the New France*. London: Routledge (1991).

Anne Stevens, *The Government and Politics of France*. London: Macmillan (1992).

Ezra Suleiman, *Elites in French Society*. Princeton, NJ: Princeton University Press (1978).

5
Parliament

Accounts of Fifth Republic politics normally dismiss Parliament as an ineffective institution that exercises little influence over the policy process and is unable – and indeed unwilling – to fulfil its basic constitutional task of controlling the executive. According to this view, the restrictions placed by the 1958 Constitution on the National Assembly mark a decisive break in the history of France's parliament, which moved virtually overnight from being one of the strongest to one of the weakest legislatures in Europe. The subsequent development of a disciplined party system inside the National Assembly served only to accentuate its subservience to government.

This analysis of Parliament's alleged impotence depends on institutional and political developments that have taken place *within* France. Yet the 'decline' in parliamentary power is a commonplace of analyses of contemporary political systems in many countries. The developing influence of parties, bureaucracies, markets and media means that parliaments everywhere have lost the power to determine policy agendas and to order governments about. Moreover, the thesis of decline and weakness depends on a particular definition of what parliaments *used* to do – and also of what they *should* do. The fact that parliaments in the French Third and Fourth Republics, in Germany's Weimar Republic, or in modern Italy found it very easy to defeat governments does not of itself prove that the political process in those countries was any more democratic than in a country like Britain where it is very rare for the House of Commons to overthrow a government.

Thus to understand the role of the National Assembly and Senate in the Fifth Republic, and to see whether its reputation for weakness is justified, we need first to set out what a parliament should do. Broadly speaking, there are four types of function:

- voting taxes;
- making laws;
- controlling government;
- debating public issues.

The Fifth Republic's assault on Parliament

The political supremacy of Parliament in the Third and Fourth Republics had three characteristics:

1. The Chamber of Deputies, which was the directly elected branch of the legislature, was the central institution in the political system and the focus of party, and pressure group, activity.
2. The sovereignty of Parliament was regarded as the indispensable condition for the existence of 'republican' democracy.
3. Parliament elected the president of the Republic, had complete control over its standing orders and over the legislative timetable; and the Chamber of Deputies made, and unmade, governments at will.

The fact that Third and Fourth Republic parliaments were powerful did not, of course, mean that they were loved. Anti-parliamentarism was a theme in French political debate long before de Gaulle denounced the vices of the *régime d'assemblée* and, in particular, the institutional imbalance that put governments at the mercy of shifting party coalitions in the

National Assembly. Curbing the role of Parliament was thus a fundamental aim of the constitutional revolution of 1958.

Chapter 2 showed that the constitutional compromise of 1958 required the Fifth Republic to acknowledge the parliamentary basis of legislation and of the government's legitimacy. Parliament – or more precisely the National Assembly – was law maker and, in specific circumstances, government unmaker. The Constitution respected the traditions of parliamentary Republicanism by providing for a bicameral legislature of National Assembly and Senate. As in earlier republics, the National Assembly sits in the Palais Bourbon and the Senate in the Palais du Luxembourg.

The present-day National Assembly contains 577 representatives – known as *deputés* (deputies). They are elected by universal suffrage and serve (provided the National Assembly runs its full term) for a five year term. The Senate contains 321 members, who represent France's mainland and overseas departments. They are not elected by universal suffrage, being chosen for a nine year term by a department-wide electoral college composed mainly of local councillors. One third of the total number is renewed every three years. As the directly elected representatives of the People, the members of the National Assembly have the final say in voting legislation and they alone can vote a government out of office. The Senate represents France's territorial collectivities (and, given that the minimum age for membership is 35, the experience that is supposed to come with age) and acts as a limited counterweight to the National Assembly. Its president becomes acting president of the Republic when there is a vacancy.

The 1958 Constitution respects the principles of parliamentary government. If de Gaulle was pathologically suspicious of the good faith of parliamentarians, his principal lieutenant Michel Debré was a great admirer of the British model of parliamentary government, and sought to create a French version of it which he called *rationalised parliamentarism*. But Debré also believed that the intensity of France's political divisions, and the fragmented party system, meant that the stable, majoritarian politics which made the Westminster system work could not be transported across the Channel. Hence it was necessary to create constitutional barriers against the disruptive activities of French parliamentarians. The result was a whole series of articles shackling the National Assembly.

The controls affect Parliament's powers (a) to make laws and (b) to unmake governments:

(a) By introducing the possibility for legislation by referendum (Article 11) and by establishing a Constitutional Council, the Fifth Republic deprives Parliament of its formal sovereignty as law maker. Constitutional Articles 34–7 define the areas in which the National Assembly legislates in detail and those in which it simply approves the outlines of a proposed law, leaving the detail to be decided by the government in the form of regulations. The National Assembly is also able to vote to hand over its law-making powers to government, which can then legislate by ordinance. The role of parliamentary committees in the legislative process has been reduced (see below) and Article 44 allows the Government to insist that only those parliamentary amendments of which it approves be included in the final vote on a bill. Article 40 limits parliamentarians' ability to influence the content of the annual Finance Bill by prohibiting ordinary deputies from proposing legislation that would increase, or decrease, public expenditure.

Yet the major restriction imposed by the Fifth Republic on the law-making freedom of the National Assembly occurs in Article 49/3. By this article the government can make parliamentary acceptance of a particular bill a matter of confidence, in which case it automatically becomes law unless a vote of censure is passed. Article 49/3 was used eight times by the Chirac government in 1986–87. More recently the Rocard/Cresson governments used it no fewer than twenty-eight times between 1988 and 1991. The net effect is that a government can pass legislation, even if there is not a majority for it in either the Senate or the

National Assembly, so long as there is not an absolute majority against it in the latter.

(b) The importance of article 49/3 is that it links constraints on law making to constraints on government unmaking. For the second way in which Parliament, and particularly the National Assembly, has been shackled is in its ability to harass government. The Constitution demonstrates de Gaulle's distrust of the irresponsibility of office-hungry parliamentarians by introducing the so-called incompatibility rule which obliges members of parliament who accept ministerial office to resign their parliamentary seat. It was hoped that this would discourage the frivolous overthrow of governments by ambitious deputies seeking to replace them.

The length of parliamentary sessions has been reduced so that the National Assembly meets for no more than five and a half months per year – the parliamentary year comprises an Autumn session that lasts for eighty days from 2 October, and is essentially devoted to passing the budget, and a 90-day Spring session starting on 2 April. Sometimes, but only when the President of the Republic agrees, sessions are extended or extraordinary sessions held – an example of the latter was the session held in January 1991 to debate and vote approval of the government's policy in the Gulf Crisis. Government controls the parliamentary timetable, and its bills (*projets de loi*) take priority over private member's proposals (*propositions de loi*). Ninety-one per cent of the 88 laws passed in 1991 originated in a government proposal.

The procedures whereby the National Assembly can overthrow a government are, unsurprisingly, much more restrictive than in earlier Republics. Only the directly elected National Assembly can force a government to resign. A motion of no confidence requires the signatures of one tenth of the members of the National Assembly, who are not allowed to sign another such motion during the rest of the parliamentary session. For the vote to be successful, it must have the support of an absolute majority of all the deputies – abstentions are effectively votes for the government.

Majority politics (le fait majoritaire)

The reason for the constraints on Parliament lies in the constitution makers' belief that unstable coalitions would continue to dominate the National Assembly and that a governmentalist party system of the British sort was impossible in France. Yet Chapter 2 showed that just such a system emerged in the Fifth Republic. What is known as *le fait majoritaire* means that parties in the National Assembly (and to a lesser extent the Senate) exist to give disciplined support to the Government – or to the potential alternative government. Instead of fragmented multipartyism, Fifth Republic National Assemblies have been dominated by *a* Majority and *an* Opposition. To be sure, each of these is a coalition of parties – but up until now it has always been a stable coalition (see Chapter 7). For most of the Fifth Republic, the two camps of Majority and Opposition have been clearly defined. Even between 1988–93, when no overall Socialist majority existed, the three governments of Rocard, Cresson and Bérégevoy always managed to put together enough parliamentary votes to avoid defeat on a vote of confidence.

It is difficult to exaggerate the importance of this development which meant that the advantages derived by government from the Constitution are supplemented by the support of a coherent parliamentary Majority. Once elected to the National Assembly, deputies join one of a number of parliamentary groups which represent the main political parties and, so long as they have twenty members, participate in the organisation of parliamentary business. Since 1962, the groups of the Majority, be it of Right or Left, have carried out the instructions of their leaders when it comes to supporting government against a vote of censure. Thus deputies and groups are no longer rivals to the government – or to the potential government; they are instead its parliamentary props.

The emergence of political discipline within the National Assembly can be seen in other ways. The six permanent committees charged with examining proposed legislation contain a majority of government supporters and are usually – as after the 1993 legislative elections – presided over by a prominent Majority spokesman. The president of the National Assembly, the equivalent of the Speaker, is elected at the start of a new legislature for the whole of its length and is always a leading member of the Majority. Though formally the spokesman of the whole house, he (there has never been a woman president) often has continuing ministerial ambition. After the 1988 elections, for example, the president was Laurent Fabius, who had been Socialist prime minister between 1984–86 and gave up his post in 1992 to become first secretary of the Socialist Party. The president of the 1993 National Assembly, a prominent neo-Gaullist politician Philippe Seguin, has used the prestige of his office to make some highly audible political pronouncements. The presidents of both houses each appoint three members to the Constitutional Council.

The case against Parliament

One of the paradoxes of Fifth Republic politics is that the constitutional and political taming of Parliament has not led to the rehabilitation of either the institution or of its members. The criticisms fall into two categories, one of legitimacy the other of effectiveness.

1. Legitimacy

Public opinion appears willing to believe that its parliamentary representatives, and particularly the deputies, protect their own interests rather than those of the electorate. Polls taken in 1992 suggested that only 25 per cent of the French have a 'good opinion' of deputies and that 46 per cent believe them to be corrupt. Some of the complaints focus on the pay and perks

which French parliamentarians enjoy. Their salary is higher
than that of their British, German and American equivalents;
they receive substantial benefits in kind such as unlimited
free first class rail travel and low-interest loans for election
campaigns and car purchases; the National Assembly recently
paid £45 million for a former hotel to provide lodgings for
deputies. More recently, there has been great controversy over
the involvement of parliamentarians in a number of high profile
corruption scandals and over the 1990 vote of an amnesty law
to protect politicians from prosecution. The tactics employed
by the majority in the 1988 Assembly to prevent the bringing
to trial of former Socialist ministers accused of malpractice led
to a media outcry.

We have seen that this type of criticism reflects a long-
standing French tradition of anti-parliamentarism, which
stretches back beyond de Gaulle's denunciations of the self- (as
opposed to the national) interest of *les politiciens* to the great
scandals of the Third Republic. To quote Stephen Bornstein
'while the French are very much impressed by the State, they
are much less impressed by politicians whom they regard as a
fundamentally dishonest and self-seeking lot regardless of their
political coloration' (Hall, Hayward, Machin 1990, p. 278). In
recent years, the Front National has made itself the spokesman
of this tradition (see Chapter 8). Yet France is far from being the
only country where such charges exist and there is less evidence
of the sort of systematic parliamentary fraud that exists in Italy.

2. *Effectiveness*

A near consensus exists among commentators that Parliament
does not properly exercise the functions that even in the Fifth
Republic it is supposed to have. The respected constitutional
expert Georges Vedel wrote in December 1991 that 'Parliament
no longer has any real role in political life' and Pierre Avril,
author of a number of studies of the French Parliament, has
spoken of the ineffectiveness of its work. The complaints
focus on its shortcomings in the areas that define a modern

legislature – supervision of legislation, control of the Executive and providing a forum for the debate of public issues.

(a) Legislation

Government dominates the law-making process. Deputies and senators are overwhelmed by the sheer volume of legislation, (the budget for example runs to 30,000 pages of text). The committee system employed to engage in line-by-line scrutiny of bills does not permit a proper analysis of proposed legislation and Parliament is unable to amend what government wants. Less than half a per cent of budget expenditure and income is modified as a result of parliamentary action.

(b) Accountability

Government is able to force through its measures via the procedural methods described above; a compliant Majority; and by offering sweeteners, in the form of constituency favours, to wavering deputies. Thus a censure motion on the Rocard government in November 1990 was backed by all the Opposition groups and also by the Communist group that was prepared, for the first time since 1957, to join its votes with the Right. The censure motion failed because nine opposition deputies from overseas departments did not support it, having received the promise of budgetary favours from the government. No censure motion has been passed since 1962.

(c) Public watchdog

Parliament does not attempt to expose the shortcomings of the Executive. Parliamentary committees of inquiry are few in number and they lack teeth: they have only six months in which to produce a report and ministers and civil servants are not required to co-operate. Their sessions are held in secret and they cannot concern themselves with issues that might give rise to legal proceedings. A procedure for questioning ministers (*questions au gouvernment*) exists: questions take place on Wednesday afternoon and are broadcast live on a public sector television channel. But question time lacks the authority of its British equivalent largely because no supplementaries are allowed; even Mitterrand criticised his Socialist ministers for failing to treat question time with sufficient seriousness. More generally, the mediatisation of political debate means that deputies much prefer to perform in a television studio than in the Palais Bourbon.

There is no equivalent of the supply days in the British parliament when the Opposition decides on the subject for debate. Such major affairs as the Greenpeace scandal of 1985 and the release of an Iranian terrorist in 1987 were barely discussed by Parliament. Critics note that, having voted approval of French participation in the Gulf War in the special session of January 1991, the National Assembly then went into recess until March and that in 1992 there was far less parliamentary debate of implications of the Maastricht Treaty on European Union than occured in Britain. Debates in the French National Assembly are often poorly attended and votes are very often cast by proxy, enabling a handful of deputies from the major parties to cast the votes of their colleagues. In the late 1980s there was much talk of a malaise in the Senate, with a very elderly president, Poher, unable, or unwilling, to deal with maladministration. (Poher was finally replaced in 1992.)

Why Parliament matters

The founding fathers of the Fifth Republic sought to weaken the political pre-eminence of the French parliament and they succeeded in doing so. Constitutional texts and political practice have combined to reduce its power. It is significant that in the greatest crisis faced by the Fifth Republic – the student and worker demonstrations of 1968 – the National Assembly was all but ignored by the protestors. More recently a 1990 demonstration of sixth formers was able to modify within two days an education budget that the deputies had been unable to change.

Yet we should note again that complaints of parliamentary impotence ignore the constraints on institutional power that are a feature of modern political systems. Some of these constraints derive from the ever-increasing interdependence of nation states and their governments; others come from the weight of past decisions on present choices in, for example, the annual budget. The criticisms also ignore the efforts made since 1974, when the Gaullist Party lost control of the presidency, to enhance the status of Parliament.

The most important institutional change was the decision to allow sixty members of either House to challenge a law that has been passed by the National Assembly, by referring it to the Constitutional Council on the grounds of unconstitutionality. This right has been extensively used in the 1980s and resulted in changes to laws passed by both Socialist and Conservative Majorities. There is an irony in the fact that an institution designed to curb Parliament's power has become a means for Opposition parliamentarians to challenge decisions of the government's parliamentary majority. By having a key role in such politically sensitive issues as the 1993 reform of the Nationality Code, which deals with the immigration issue, the Constitutional Council acts as a form of lightning conductor, taking political pressure off the National Assembly.

The Assembly has in recent years shown more initiative in seeking to amend government legislation; and governments have taken more account of its views. That this should be so reflects changing political circumstances. Between 1981–86 and 1988–93 the Assembly was dominated by the Socialist Party, which has a broader view of the rights of parliamentarians than did the Gaullists. The 1986–88 cohabitation period and the absence after 1988 of an overall government majority in the National Assembly gave a wider margin of manoeuvre to deputies. Thus 82 per cent of the 2285 amendments made to the 61 laws promulgated in 1989 originated in parliamentary committees or groups. Whereas in 1969 only 1000 amendments were proposed to government bills, the equivalent figure in 1990 was 8503. The six permanent committees of the National Assembly have begun to set up joint sub-committees to examine particular topics and have also established investigative missions dealing with policy areas (e.g. the Finance Committee report on Economic and Monetary Union). Nine committees of enquiry were established by the 1988 Assembly. The 1993 president of the National Assembly, Philippe Seguin is, like his Gaullist predecessor Michel Debré, an admirer of British parliamentary procedures; unlike Debré he regards this as requiring a more positive assertion of deputies' rights to interrogate the Executive.

If neither house has been completely quiescent in its relations with government, the Senate has been more – and surprisingly – effective. The Constitution makers' hope that the Senate would act as a useful counterweight to a turbulent 'lower house' has not been realised. In the first decade of the Fifth Republic, the Senate, and particularly its energetic president Gaston Monnerville, became an irritating – if ultimately impotent – thorn in the flesh of the new regime and so infuriated de Gaulle that in 1969 he sought by referendum to reform it out of existence. The new Senate President, Alain Poher, played an important role in ensuring the defeat of the referendum and bringing about de Gaulle's resignation in 1969. After the victory of the Left in 1981, the Senate once more became a centre of opposition to government, despite the latter's ostentatious respect for its status as representative of the territorial collectivities, when drawing up plans for local government reform. It also used one of the few prerogatives which it shares with the National Assembly – the power to amend the constitution – to defeat Mitterrand's constitutional proposals in 1984 and 1990. In 1992 the Senate was enabled to extract concessions over the constitutional changes made necessary by the Maastricht Treaty.

A characteristic of some Fifth Republic governments is the relatively high proportion of ministers who, when appointed, are not members of either Senate or Chamber. De Gaulle's governments contained a high number of top civil servants and the 1962 appointment as prime minister of Pompidou, who had never been an MP, was widely interpreted as a deliberate snub to the National Assembly. To the unrealistic Gaullist desire to 'depoliticise' government can be added the French confidence in the technical expert (or media star) and the suspicion of the political class as reasons for the appointment of non-parliamentarians to government office. Yet France's political class continue to regard a parliamentary seat as a vital part of their career development. Even de Gaulle instructed all his ministers to contest the 1967 National Assembly elections. With the exception of the Communist Party and *Front National*, leadership positions in all the political parties are held by parliamentarians. Ministers may acquire their original reputation in business, a profession or the civil service but the example of Raymond Barre, who became a Lyons deputy in 1978 eighteen months after becoming prime minister, shows the political importance of a parliamentary base. Many members of the public service elite have exchanged their administrative posts for elective office. The career of Philippe Seguin shows how a political reputation can be built on effective parliamentary performances and the example of Bernard Tapie shows that even a business superstar can want the glory that comes from membership of, if not attendance at, the National Assembly.

More fundamentally, parliament establishes the parameters of government action and, in times of cohabitation, the limits to presidentialism (Wright 1989, p. 149). Be it ever so powerful, the government can only do what the National Assembly will tolerate. During the latter part of his presidency, Giscard d'Estaing and his prime minister Barre faced difficulties in getting bills through a National Assembly where his parliamentary majority included a powerful, and ill-tempered, neo-Gaullist group. After 1988 the Socialist-led governments lacked an overall majority and were consequently obliged to give up some of their proposals and to bargain with groups that are not part of its coalition. In 1991 two important bills, on reform of the legal professions and on profit sharing, had to be withdrawn in the face of parliamentary opposition.

The representativeness of Parliament and parliamentarians

Representativeness (or its absence) can be defined in various ways. The number of women deputies is lower in present-day France than it was in the Fourth Republic, when women had only just received the vote. Only 32 women were elected to the National Assembly in 1993. The average deputy is male, middle aged, and middle class; France's immigrant community is unrepresented and there are hardly any deputies from the working class. The strength of parties in the National Assembly is a very imperfect reflection of their overall electoral position. In 1993 the parties of the Right won 80 per cent of the seats with 40 per cent of the first-round vote; five years earlier the Socialists and their allies gained nearly half the seats with 36 per cent of the round-one vote (see Chapter 8).

Such sociological and political imbalances are commonplace in modern legislatures everywhere and they do not of themselves produce a crisis of representative legitimacy. The fact that over 5000 candidates stood for election to the 1993 National Assembly election and that 69 per cent of the electorate turned out to vote does not suggest that parliamentarians are regarded as pariahs. The many critics of the undemocratic nature of French institutions always argue that parliament's powers should be increased, not that they should be abolished.

It is also noteworthy that, despite the fact that French MPs are so frequently accused of an improper interest in their individual well-being, their electors continue to have high expectations of the services they should receive from them. Though formally the representatives (*élus*) of the Nation, the deputies' most important role can often seem to be that of intermediary between their constituents and the Administration. In December 1990 twelve deputies, from parties of both Right and Left, wrote an article for *Le Monde* newspaper entitled 'deputies and proud to be so' in which they defended the honorability of their profession and cited the services it could render to ordinary citizens. Constituents expect their MPs to intervene on their behalf with local and central government. Thus much of a deputy's time is spent writing letters to the relevant administration seeking some sort of favour for an individual citizen; he or she becomes in effect a sort of social worker. The requests cover an enormous range of topics – from work permits, requests for jobs in the public sector, study grants and council housing to pleas for exemption from military service; for the return of confiscated driving licences or the quashing of traffic offence fines to the award of a decoration. It has been calculated that central government departments receive a total of about 60,000 letters every year from MPs – for local authorities the figure is certainly much higher.

Many of these interventions will have no effect whatsoever. The fact that they continue to be made, however, shows the symbolic importance of the *élu* as the link between an often remote administration and the ordinary individual. The French complain about their deputies – but they also regard them as an essential element in the humanising of a system that is based on the impersonal authority of the State.

Conclusion

Before 1958 parliament was accused of making effective government impossible. In the Fifth Republic it is written off as an irrelevance. The latter claim reflects both the emergence of *le fait majoritaire* as the dominant principle in French parliamentary politics and the constitutional constraints placed on the National Assembly. It does not necessarily imply that French parliamentarians are indifferent to their role as legislators, as controllers of government or, importantly, as representatives of their constituencies. A parliamentary seat continues to be an important resource for the politically ambitious. Above all, the National Assembly still determines whether the President or Prime Minister will be the leading political actor; and if the disciplined party system that has operated since 1962 were to break down then its potential for disruption would be great.

The fact remains that neither Senate nor National Assembly have succeeded in convincing their critics of the effectiveness of their role. Parliament's claim to be the sole 'voice of the French Nation' was unconvincing even before the Fifth Republic rejected it outright in constitutional text and political practice. Thirty years after the 1962 amendment on the direct election of the presidency, there is not much evidence that the National Assembly has regained its lost power. Fortunately for it, and for the system, there is even less sign that public opinion seeks a return to the *régime d'assemblée* of the Fourth Republic.

6

Local government in a centralised state

To the British student of French politics, one of the most notable changes of recent years is the series of laws passed by the Socialist government of the early 1980s organising relationships between local and central government. It is true that British local government has also undergone many changes in recent years. But whereas in Britain the purpose of change has been to restrict the powers and resources of local councils, in France the goal was completely different. It was to increase the power of elected local authorities and to put an end to the centuries-old tradition of centralisation that has kept them in an apparent state of subordination to, and dependency on, central government. The 1980s reforms were described, in a phrase that has become famous, as the principal business (*la grande affaire*) of Mitterrand's first presidency and are now firmly entrenched in practice.

But what has the new legislation actually changed in the relationship between local government authorities and French national government? To answer this question we need to look at three issues:

1. the theory and practice that underpinned central-local relations before the 1980s;
2. the rationale and content of the 1980s legislation;
3. the effect of the laws on the various levels of local government in France – and also on central government.

Theory and Practice

Theory

France has always been viewed – and has often been criticised – as one of the most centralised states in Europe. Centralisation defines a spatial distribution and organisation of power. It means first that legal decision-taking authority is concentrated in a single, 'nation-representing' institution, as it is in the United Kingdom. For ideological and historical reasons, American-style federalism is completely absent from the French model of territorial administration. It has been rejected as a threat to the citizen equality of the nation, and as a strategy advocated at various times in the nineteenth and twentieth centuries by Right-wing and Left-wing groups to destroy the political order established by the French Revolution.

But there is more to French centralisation than the concentration of political authority in a single institution. It also implies that the central government should control the organisation and content of public services provided for the community. The model presupposes administrative uniformity and assumes that such 'sub-national' authorities as do exist will have very limited autonomy and will be subject to continuous supervision by agents of central government. An example of what French centralisation can mean is the education system (see Chapter 5). All French sixth formers take the same State-organised examination, the *baccalaureat*; all university students who pass their exams are awarded a national degree; the educational role of local authorities is very circumscribed.

Thus the British tradition of devolving government functions on to local elites and of tolerating different forms of local administration is absent. The differing traditions that structure the relationship between centre and periphery in France and Britain can be seen in various ways. The mayor of a French commune is regarded as an official of the State, and the symbol of her or his authority is a sash in the colours of the national flag, rather than, as in Britain, a municipal mace. Uniformity characterises France's local government structures rather than the administrative pluralism existing in the United Kingdom. What we call 'France' includes territories in the West Indies and Indian Ocean as well as a European land mass that stretches from the Pyrenees to the Belgian border. The uniform local government structures which operate throughout this vast territory, and for which the term 'territorial administration' is employed, obviously contrast with the variety of organisation existing in the United Kingdom, where Scotland for example has its own legal system and administration.

Although the nineteenth-century political sociologist Alexis de Tocqueville argued that French centralisation pre-dates 1789, the territorial structures with which it is identified date from the Revolution. At that time the existing units of local government – parish and province – were swept away and replaced by two basic units, commune and department. There are today some 36,750 communes and a hundred departments, ninety-six in mainland France, four overseas. Both communes and departments differ enormously in size and economic wealth. Yet every commune, be it Paris or a tiny rural settlement lost in the Limousin, is run by an elected council (*conseil municipal*), headed by a mayor, and every department possesses an elected *conseil général*, headed by a president. Within each department, two other administrative units – cantons and *arrondissements* – exist and in 1977, as we shall see, the departments were grouped together into twenty-two regions.

The creation of communes testifies to the original goal of the Revolution to transfer power to the People; but the geographical organisation of the departments shows the revolutionary concern to treat the French people as citizens of one nation rather than as inhabitants of different regions. The cultural and political identity of France's traditional provinces was denied by creating departments of roughly equal size and giving them names that derived exclusively from physical and geographical features. Departmental boundaries were fixed so that mounted troops could get to and from the administrative centre (*chef lieu*) to any part of the territory in two days. From their creation, communes had statutory responsibilities in the area of public order and health.

This concern to obliterate identities that were not national was strengthened by the realisation that the regional diversity of France was not politically neutral – Catholic areas like Brittany long remained hostile to the revolutionary settlement – and by central government's anxiety that any relaxation of its control on the national territory would threaten regime stability. Governments' fear of Paris, the revolutionary city par excellence, was particularly strong. In 1871 a bloody uprising known as the Commune, and an even bloodier repression, took place in Paris. As a result, France's capital city was not allowed to govern itself or even to elect a mayor; it was run instead by officials of central government under the aegis of the Minister of the Interior. When critics denounced the excessive weight of Paris in the economic and political life of the country, they were emphatically not referring to the feeble institutions that the city possessed.

The political and administrative subordination of the localities to the Centre was entrenched by legislation. It is true that in the 1880s laws were passed providing for the election of municipal and departmental councils by male universal suffrage. But this did not alter the formal bases of their dependency. Legal and administrative subordination was symbolised by the existence of an official (the prefect) and a legal term (*tutelle*).

The prefect – an official created by Napoleon – represented the State in the department. Possessing extensive supervisory powers over elected local government officials and chief executives of the departmental council, the prefects were appointed by central government and were responsible to it alone. They were not the only agents of central power – the Finance Ministry had its own officials, the *trésoriers payeurs généraux*, in every department – but they were the most visible.

The legal term *tutelle* defined the relationship between State and local authorities. In law *tutelle* defines the relationship between a guardian and a minor, that is to say somebody who is not fully responsible for her or his actions. The *tutelle* meant that all decisions of local authorities were subject to the prior approval of the State, via its representative the prefect.

Practice

The prefects are often portrayed as centralisation made flesh. They have no real equivalent in Britain, where the representative of the Crown, the lord lieutenant, appears to spend much of his time shaking the hands of visiting members of the Royal Family. Yet the reality of central–local relations always differed from the pattern laid down by ideological tradition and administrative texts. A substantial literature exists showing the mutual interests and dependencies that characterised relations between Paris and the localities, and the inadequacy of the 'power-dependency' model of French local government. Two developments in particular are important:

(a) The democratisation of local government in the Third Republic meant that municipal and departmental councils came to be dominated by groups of influential local figures known as the *notables*. The term notable crops up constantly in analyses of French local and national politics – past and present – and is not easy to define in English. Pierre Gremion, one of France's leading experts on central–local relations, defines the notable as 'a man [sic] who disposes of power to act on the State apparatus at certain key levels and whose own political power is reinforced as a result of these contacts for so long as they produce results'. The notables used their social and professional position to acquire local office and were able to bargain their support with central government, which needed their co-operation for its own programmes of economic and social improvement – and also to maintain overall political stability. Even the 'anti-system' French Communist Party was able to use local government to construct bastions of support in the 1920s and 1930s, something it could not have done if the town halls were as weak as the legend suggests.

(b) The concept of the notable and his influence derives from
     the France of small towns and villages that existed until
     the 1950s. Starting in the 1950s, a process of massive
     urbanisation has transformed existing regional centres like
     Grenoble, Lyons, Bordeaux, and Montpellier and created
     a whole series of new towns and suburbs, mainly but not
     exclusively in the Paris region. What is significant is that the
     existing structures and relationships survived the change.
     In the 1960s the phenomenon of multiple office-holding
     – the *cumul des mandats* – became widespread. Prominent
     politicians of all parties became very keen to acquire
     local as well as national mandates and the number of
     deputy-mayors soared. Amongst the most celebrated were
     Chaban-Delmas (Bordeaux), Lecanuet (Rouen), Defferre
     (Marseilles), d'Ornano (Deauville), Dubedout (Grenoble),
     Faure (Cahors), and Laurent and Mauroy (Lille). That
     important national figures belonging to the Opposition as
     well as the Majority wanted to hold local office proves
     once again that local government was not as powerless
     as the myth of the centralised state and the post-war
     image of 'Paris and the French Desert' would suggest.
     Howard Machin's 1977 study *The Prefect in Modern France*
     shows clearly that prefects were far from being the jack-
     booted masters of local government and that they were
     susceptible to the influence of well-entrenched local no-
     tables. Government concern that these so-called agents
     of the national interest might actually become lobbyists
     for local pressures explains why they were frequently
     shifted around; the average length of stay of a prefect in
     a department was only thirty months.

It might be expected that the advent of the Fifth Republic
would have led to a radical restructuring of local government,
given that institutional reorganisation in the name of national
efficiency was the hallmark of de Gaulle's ambitions for France.
A number of innovations were carried out in the 1960s and
1970s:

1. a new body, the *Délégation à l'Aménagement du Territoire et à l'Action Regionale*, was created to encourage, and control, regional economic development;
2. five new departments were created in the Paris region in the early 1960s;
3. a number of urban communities (*communautés urbaines*) were formed to group services provided by existing communes;
4. a 1972 law added a new layer of local government by establishing twenty-two regions;
5. in 1977 Paris acquired a mayor for the first time in over a century, thus giving it the same status as France's 36,000 other communes;
6. the financial *tutelle* on local government decisions was weakened.

These reforms did not however challenge the existing bases of local government. No attempt was made by government to impose a reduction in the number of communes, many of which had tiny populations and were incapable of improving the services they provided, or to amalgamate the more economically backward departments. The new regions created in 1972 had very restricted powers of economic intervention. Their councils were supervised by a regional prefect and were not elected by universal suffrage. The continuing fear that a strong regional identity in Catholic Brittany might threaten national unity led to the non-inclusion of the department containing the region's historic capital, Nantes, in the new Brittany region.

The limited nature of reform by governments that were, in other sectors, highly interventionist shows the tenacity of France's local government structures and contrasts with the British changes in the 1970s. There is a striking contrast between the instability of France's national political institutions and the durability of its local government. The most radical proposal, de Gaulle's 1969 attempt to weaken the power base of the Senate, which acted as spokesman for local authorities, was defeated in a referendum. Its failure was interpreted as showing the attachment of the French to the existing order. The Fifth Republic also showed that centralisation did not prevent dynamic local leaders from carrying out programmes of urban development and establishing large bureaucracies in their city halls, and that it also provided small councils with the technical resources they needed, thus protecting them from being swallowed up by more powerful neighbours. It is a fact that 500,000 French men and women are members of a municipal council.

The 1980s reforms

For all their solidity, there was by the late 1970s widespread acceptance that the existing local government structures were in need of a reform that would bring decision-taking closer to the communities over whom it was exercised. Except in a few, mainly Gaullist, circles the attraction of centralisation had waned. There are three reasons for this:

1. The formal centralisation of the system meant that the procedures involved in obtaining official approval for local government projects were often extraordinarily complex and time-consuming. A leading Gaullist, Alain Peyrefitte, who was also mayor of a town outside Paris, wrote a bestselling book *Le Mal Français* that described and denounced the blockages in the system.
2. One of the consequences of the 1968 disturbances was a growing interest in *autogestion* (self-management). It was felt, and not only on the Left, that giving more responsibility to local communities would make for a freer, and more united, national community as well as a more efficient one. Part of this new self-responsibility would derive from reducing the bureaucratic dependency of local authorities on the central administration.
3. By the end of the 1970s the parties of the Left had won control of two-thirds of France's towns with a population of more than 30,000. Socialists and Communists believed

that there was much political advantage to be derived from extending local government powers which could be used to provide services that would in turn create strong electoral loyalties based on patronage.

After their 1981 victory, the Socialists moved fast to implement their proposals. Reform was entrusted to a veteran Socialist politician Gaston Defferre, whose career as long-time mayor of Marseilles was living proof that the existing system was not powerless and who now took on the office of Minister of the Interior and of Decentralisation. In 1982 a framework law was passed setting out a new organisation of executive powers between the various levels of local government. Twenty-two subsequent laws and 170 decrees organised the transfer of functions and resources from centre to locality.

The reforms affected three areas.

1. The organisation of local government power

Executive power was transferred in department and region from the prefects to the presidents of the departmental and regional councils. The prefect's *a priori tutelle* over the administrative acts and budgets of mayors was abolished and replaced with an *a posteori* judicial system of review over the financial activities of local governments carried out by a Regional Court of Accounts. The official title of prefect was replaced by that of Commissioner of the Republic. Regional councils were henceforth to be elected by universal suffrage, with the department as the constituency. For communes with more than 3500 inhabitants an element of proportional representation was introduced, with opposition lists for the first time being given a number of seats on the municipal council. A recent (1991) law provides that in future departmental councils will be elected every six years in their entirety rather than, as at present, half the members being elected every three years.

In order to broaden involvement in the system and to prevent political grandees using – and abusing – their connections, a limit was placed on the number of elected positions that an individual could hold. A 1985 law restricted to two the 'significant' elected offices a member of parliament may hold.

2. The tasks/responsibilities of local government authorities

Each level of local government was given a range of responsibilities:

(a) The regional councils have charge of regional economic planning and policy, industrial development and professional education and training and they participate in the elaboration of the national Plan. They are able to offer financial support to companies in their region, so long as the latter are not in difficulty, and are responsible for the building and maintenance of high schools (lycées);

(b) The departmental councils are responsible for the delivery of health and social services, construction and maintenance of public thoroughfares, school bus transportation and the construction and upkeep of secondary schools (colleges);

(c) The municipal councils are now entitled to draw up their own land-use plans (POS) and to grant building permits.

All levels of local authority, not just the regions, were given new powers to intervene in the local economy and assist local industries either directly or indirectly by means of loans, grants and tax concessions.

3. Transfer of resources

Each transfer of function from centre to locality has been funded by an equivalent transfer of cash, and the proceeds of a number of national taxes (e.g. car registration) have been handed over *en bloc* to local authorities. Local authorities now have complete autonomy over a number of taxes, including those on property and businesses. As of 1987, departments and regions gained the freedom to set the rate of local taxes. Two large block grants – for capital investment and the operating costs of decentralisation – were created and educational and cultural funds were also made available. Administrative personnel in the affected areas was transferred from central to local government.

The impact of the reforms: change, continuity, problems

French government is now considerably less centralised than it was when the Socialists came to power (Hall, Hayward, Machin 1990, p. 167). The presidents of regional and departmental councils enjoy the same executive authority as mayors and some 120,000 officials have been transferred from (State-run) prefectures to regional and departmental authorities. The departmental councils have major responsibilities in the areas of health and social security. Local authorities spend 10 per cent of gross domestic product and employ 1.2 million workers. The departmental councils have major responsibilities in the areas of health and social security and there has been a considerable expansion in the ambitions of regional councils. The Rhône-Alpes region has taken the lead in opening a representative office in Brussels and has signed a co-operation pact with Lombardy, Catalonia and Baden Wurtemberg, the so-called 'four motors of Europe'.

The Defferre reforms have been widely accepted. Though passed during the most ideologically ambitious period of the Socialist presidency, they were hardly modified by the government of Jacques Chirac (1986–88), mainly because the right-wing parties had made major gains in local and regional elections. One of the changes was symbolic – a return to the traditional title of prefect – and the other involved a restoration of the *tutelle* of the Finance Ministry over the finances of small communes.

It is easy to say that decentralisation is by definition popular since it brings power closer to the people. Yet it is far from clear that the Defferre reforms have encouraged greater democratic participation in the running of local government or weakened the power of existing elites. The percentage of deputy mayors reached new heights in the 1980s and fell back in 1993 only because of the scale of the electoral defeat of the Socialist Party. The mayor and the notable continue to be the key players and the phenomenon of the *cumulard*, for all that the number of offices that can be held simultaneously has been reduced to two, is as strong as ever.

What this suggests is that the reforms have worked because they have worked with the grain of existing structures and practices rather than against it and because they have not overturned the rights of existing authorities. The visible – and popular – role of the mayor as leader of her or his community has been enhanced and the Socialists were no more ready than their conservative predecessors to reform out of existence the 28,000 communes with less than 1000 inhabitants. The creation of regional councils has not weakened municipal or departmental authority, since their resources are only 12 per cent of those available to municipalities.

Continuities also exist in other areas. The reforms have in no sense transformed France into a quasi-federal state. Chapter 1 noted that the Constitutional Council refused to allow any reference to the 'Corsican people' in a recent law establishing special arrangements for Corsica. Another sign of this enduring suspicion of powerful regional identities is that the regional councillors are elected by individual departments rather than by a single region-wide constituency and that the Loire Atlantique department, containing Nantes, is still not included in the Brittany region. The importance of the prefects and of other central government officials has not disappeared. That many of them have taken up senior positions in big city, departmental and regional councils shows that local government is attractive to high fliers – but also that the new structures will be imbued with existing administrative styles.

The local press still pays much attention to the activities of the prefect and his assistants (for example when they arbitrate in local disputes) and in rural areas mayors of small communes continue to rely on the technical, and financial, services provided by the Administration. Thus the prefects continue to protect small authorities, who also welcomed the Chirac government's partial restoration of the financial *tutelle* as being preferable to investigation by the regional Courts of Account. The prefect continues to be responsible for ensuring the overall security of her or his department and he or she usefully (so far as local government is concerned) carries the can when things go wrong. In May 1992 the prefect of Upper Corsica was sacked shortly after the Furiani football stadium disaster.

One policy area – public sector education – that in Britain was until recently dominated by local government remains under State control in France. Central government controls the organisation of the teaching profession, and decides on the content of the curriculum and the way it is to be taught. Local government is responsible for school buildings, but neither it nor parents' associations can determine what schooling will be like. More generally the financial dependence of all levels of local government on central government grant remains huge. Local expenditure has of course risen because of the transfer of resources and responsibilities; but much of this is effectively committed in advance for the enactment of nationally decided policies.

An argument used by those who were against the spirit of the Defferre laws was that the removal of the *a priori tutelle* of the central administration would lead to financial malpractice and corruption. It was claimed that the unsupervised right to issue planning permissions and so on would enable local political bosses to enrich themselves and the parties they support. Such claims derive in part from the generalised suspicion of politicians' honesty that we have already noted in Chapter 5. They reflect, too, resentment at the lavish facilities with which some councils have equipped themselves and at the high expenses councillors can receive; the salary of a departmental councillor varies from 31,000 francs in Correze to 257,000 in the Hauts de Seine. As mayor of

Paris, Chirac has been able to construct a highly effective patronage system based on the use of municipal contracts, housing etc.

Evidence certainly exists that decentralisation has increased the existing possibilities for municipal corruption. A number of spectacular affairs have surfaced, most notably in Angoulême, (46,000 inhabitants), where the (ex-Socialist) deputy Boucheron ran up municipal debts that effectively bankrupted the city and in Nice, where the long-time mayor Jean Médecin engaged in systematic corruption. Both Boucheron and Médecin fled into exile in South America. Yet the long history of the Médecin family in Nice shows that there is nothing new in municipal corruption. What has caused much controversy are cases in which local party bosses trade favourable planning decisions and municipal contracts in return for contributions to electoral and other party funds. As the governing party, the Socialists suffered particularly badly in the 1993 elections from one such case, the Urba Technic affair, which first surfaced in the 1980s.

A 1991 law established the principle that a proportion of the resources of France's richest communes should be diverted to the poorest ones. But deep inequalities remain between rich cities and impoverished suburbs and between affluent and poor regions, the latter being concentrated in France's decaying agricultural and industrial regions. The Ile de France region (Paris and its surrounding departments) has 2.2 per cent of the national territory, 18.8 per cent of the national population, 25.9 per cent of total household income and 78 per cent of the headquarters of France's 200 biggest companies. The department of the Hauts de Seine alone has a GDP greater than that of Greece. The region, however, also contains departments – Val de Marne, Seine Saint Denis – that have experienced widespread economic and social deprivation. The example of the Ile de France shows that economic and cultural centralisation remain, and may even be accentuated, by the localising of political decision-taking.

Conclusion

The distribution of power between centre and periphery has not been revolutionised in recent years. The prefect retains his role as representative of the State, central government still has a preponderant interest in major policy areas like education, and the mayor continues to dominate the municipal council. Yves Mény is thus right to conclude that 'the reform, far from leading to the dismantling of the State, is rather an element of the consensual integration which associates local elites with the administration, while marginalising the most radical nationalist or regionalist dissenters' (quoted in Hall, Hayward, Machin 1990, p. 167).

The point is, however, that 'dismantling the State' was not the intention of the reform and that separatist, or even regionalist, dissent is not widespread in present-day France. With the partial exception of Corsica, France has not experienced the 'crisis of the State' that exists in Northern Ireland. The urban unrest which manifests itself in periodic outbreaks of violence in the run-down suburbs of many big cities is not inspired by any separatist project. Critics of the Defferre laws argue that they have entrenched a series of local government fiefdoms and that the costs of local government are dangerously high. Their defenders claim that the new powers enable local government to respond effectively to the needs of their communities and that the role of the regional Court of Accounts in scrutinising the budgets of cities and departments has acted as a deterrent to the sorts of abuses that they uncovered in Nice and Angoulême.

There does appear to be overall satisfaction with the existing structures, and style, of central–local relations. Turn-out at elections for municipal, and even regional councils, approaches 70 per cent, a far higher figure than that found in the United Kingdom. Such figures show that the French public believes that local government does make a difference and is interested in what councils do. Civic and departmental identities are strong. The co-operation that defines relationships between local authorities and central government also brings administration closer to the administered. Thus local government brings an element of integration to a system supposedly marked by institutional fragility, authoritarian government and voter scepticism about the political process.

Further reading

Vivien Schmidt, *Democratising France*. Cambridge: Cambridge University Press (1991).

7
The bases of party politics

A competitive party system is central to the political and societal pluralism that defines liberal democracy. Parties organise the competition for votes which creates the democratic link between government and governed; they help to determine the agenda on which electoral and policy choices are made; and they provide a political system with most of its governing personnel. This chapter looks at the development of the French party system and assesses the impact of the Fifth Republic on existing patterns of party organisation and competition.

Multipartyism and the 'Two Frances'

The history of French party politics is complicated. The principal elements of democratic politics emerged very early. Universal male suffrage came sooner than almost anywhere else – the principle was asserted in 1793, the practice definitively established in 1848 – and France is a country that votes often. There have been only seven years since 1958 when the entire electorate was not invited to vote in a presidential, parliamentary, local or (since 1979) European election.

The organising categories of modern adversarial politics – Right and Left – date, as Chapter 1 showed, from the Revolution and have given an apparent stability to French political choice. A clear, and enduring, electoral geography emerged in the nineteenth century so that it became possible to identify departments and regions as voting consistently 'Right' or 'Left'. The role of religion has been particularly important in shaping electoral outcomes. In the past, the conflict between clericals and anti-clericals was regarded as the basic cleavage within French politics and even today, as Frears says, 'where the Catholic Church is strongest the vote for the Left is weakest' (Frears 1991, p. 132). The belief that France is somehow politically cut into two – 'les deux Frances' – is reinforced by these long-standing patterns of electoral choice.

Yet if elections came early in France, political parties developed late. Elsewhere, mass parties, based on the emerging urban industrial workers, built nationwide organisations to fight for the right to representation in parliament. In France the vote pre-dated widespread industrialisation and urbanisation; the bulk of the electorate were peasants; and elections were dominated by the urban bourgeoisie or by rural notables. With the exception of a few socialist organisations, 'modern' political parties did not emerge until the first years of the twentieth century. Even after their emergence, party discipline was weak and many deputies had only a tenuous loyalty to the parties to which they formally belonged.

Multipartyism is a dominant characteristic of political organisation. France has never acquired the two-party politics familiar to Britain and the United States. Political choice may be structured around the two traditions of 'Right' and 'Left', but both 'Right' and 'Left' are, as we shall see, composed of different groupings. No one party has ever gained a majority of votes cast; only twice in the Fifth Republic (1968 and 1981) has a single party won an absolute majority of National Assembly seats; and such periods of single-party dominance have been short-lived. Thus the Gaullist Party's share of the national vote fell from 37.3 per cent to 15.4 per cent between the 1968 parliamentary elections and the 1974 presidential contest and the Socialist Party's electorate declined from eight to four million between the parliamentary elections of 1988 and 1993.

French electoral law acknowledges, and encourages, the inevitability of multipartyism. Presidential contests have always been two-round affairs, given that election on round one requires the successful candidate to have an absolute majority of votes cast. Elections for the National Assembly are contested either by proportional representation or (the dominant system in the Fifth Republic) a two-ballot system in which candidates need an overall majority, as opposed to a simple plurality of votes cast, to be elected on round one. The majority of National Assembly seats are always decided on round two. In the four most recent parliamentary elections held on the two-ballot system, the total number of seats won on the first round was 68 (1978), 156 (1981), 119 (1988) and 80 (1993).

As well as the voting system, the different types of French elections – municipal, departmental, regional, parliamentary, presidential, European – encourage multipartyism by enabling smaller parties to maintain a presence in some contests even if they cannot hope to win the major battles. In recent years the use of a nationwide proportional representation system for European elections and (in 1986) for the National Assembly has had the same effect.

Multipartyism cannot, however, be explained solely in terms of electoral law since it reflects enduring characteristics of the party culture.

1.   French parties have always been weak in terms of membership and resources. The French political scientist Michel Duverger drew a distinction between mass and *cadre* parties, the former being disciplined and programme-based organisations linking parliamentarians and activists, and the latter loosely organised coalitions of political leaders without any mass membership or strong programmatic identity. Examples of the former are the French Communist Party (PCF), the Socialist Party (PS) and the Gaullist parties of the Fourth and Fifth Republic. Even these parties have been prone to splits, however, and their membership figures did not match those of equivalent mass parties in Britain, Italy or

Germany. *Cadre* parties include the bulk of the parties of the Third and Fourth Republics and the non-Gaullist Centre parties in the Fifth Republic. The financial scandals that are an endemic element of French party politics indicate the inability of parties to mobilise a mass base.

Voter loyalty to individual parties is relatively low and the fact that most French elections go to two rounds means that many voters will in any case cast their vote for candidates of more than one party. Since 1974 the publication of opinion polls has been banned in the last stages of election campaigns, a prohibition that reflects not only suspicion of the politicisation of some polling organisations, but also the fact that sections of the electorate identify weakly with one party and are susceptible to bandwagons. It is by no means unusual for politicians to change allegiance from one party to another and the determination with which MPs in all parties try to acquire a local government base (see Chapter 6) shows the ineffectiveness of party label as electoral mobiliser. There is a tradition of so-called 'flash parties' emerging out of nowhere to challenge the existing party system; Chapter 8 will show how new parties have emerged in the 1980s to challenge the hegemony of the established ones. For all these reasons, it is not surprising that Yves Mény uses the metaphor of a volcano to describe the party landscape or that Machin refers to it as intrinsically changing and changeable (Hall, Hayward, Machin 1990, p. 33).

2. Parties possess weak representative legitimacy. Whereas in Britain and the United States they are the principal organisers of the democratic process, a well-established tradition in France regards them as its enemies. The suspicion reflects, once again, the universalist claims made about French democracy and the belief that any 'sub-national' group is potentially a conspiracy against the General Interest. Chapter 2 showed that de Gaulle denounced the *régime des partis* of the Fourth Republic and to this day Gaullist organisations reject the use of

the word party, using instead the all-embracing terms 'rassemblement' (rally) or union. But it is not only on the Right that 'antipartyism' exists. French trade unionism has always rejected the organic links with a party that developed between the British Labour Party and the Trade Unions. Chapter 3 showed that although party management is a necessary part of presidential activity, Fifth Republic presidents do not attend conferences of the party from which they emerge.

Thus 'Party government' does not convey the idea of the legitimate rule of the elected majority. In the Fourth Republic it suggested corrupt concordats worked out in smoke-filled rooms by the political bosses who made and unmade weak coalition governments. In the Fifth Republic, it has implied the arrogant abuse of State patronage by dominant parties, like the Gaullists in the 1960s and early 1970s and the Socialists in the late 1980s. Opposition parties ritualistically complain of such abuses; and with equal inevitability new governments (e.g. Balladur in 1993) start out by saying that they will put an end to political patronage.

3. The apparent simplicity of the 'two Frances' model of political choice has always concealed a variety of ideological positions and party allegiance. Issues of regime form and the proper place of the Catholic Church produced antagonisms that complement the 'classic' cleavages of social class. The core distinction between Right and Left enabled groups from within both camps to come together at key moments in the political calendar, like the second round of elections, against the common enemy. But such agreements were based on tradition and tactics rather than on a common programme or a durable coalition.

To understand the French system, it is therefore useful to think of a number of political families on both Left and Right, each appealing to an ideological tradition and to one, or several, social categories.

Political families in France

The Left

(*a*) *The Republican Left.* Republicanism is identified with the Radical Party, founded in 1901 at the time of the Dreyfus Affair. The principle of Radical republicanism was the defence of the parliamentary Republic, and the principles of the French Revolution, against their right-wing enemies. It had an anti-clerical, egalitarian and socially progressive programme based on the doctrine of the rights of man and the citizen and on Jacobin patriotism. Its vision of the good society was of a property-owning democracy rather than the emancipation of the proletariat, and it opposed Marxist theories of the expropriation of property and the inevitability of class conflict. Over time the Radical Party became identified with the defence of the rural middle classes against redistributive taxation and economic modernisation. It lost its progressive image and – after 1958 – almost all its electorate. But the theme of republicanism continues to feature in left-wing discourse, and 'republican discipline' is the term used to describe the second-round voting agreements between the parties of the Left.

(*b*) *The Socialist Left.* The Socialist Party (SFIO) was founded in 1905 out of a number of pre-existing socialist parties and with an inspirational leader, Jean Jaurès. The SFIO had a Marxist programme that rejected bourgeois reformism and private property in the name of collectivism and social transformation. It acquired a strong base among sections of France's industrial proletariat, minor civil servants and teachers and depressed peasantry and in 1936, for the first time, its leaders came to office. For all its doctrinal Marxism, the SFIO shared the Radicals' commitment to the parliamentary Republic, to anti-clericalism and to Jacobin patriotism. The appeal of the SFIO was badly compromised by its leaders' actions in the governments of the Fourth Republic and it suffered numerous splits. Yet Socialism remained the principal vehicle of the democratic Left and we shall see that in the 1970s the Socialist Party (PS) experienced a spectacular recovery.

(*c*) *The Communist Left.* A tradition of revolutionary politics persisted throughout the nineteenth century and periodically erupted on to the political scene, notably during the 1871 Paris Commune. The French Communist Party (PCF) was founded in 1920 to promote the revolutionary principles of Lenin's Third International. French Communists spoke the language of the class struggle, the revolutionary expropriation of capital and the leading role of the Party. Their patriotism was that of the international working class and its homeland, the Soviet Union, and they denounced the republican patriotism of Radicals and Socialists as a new form of opium for the masses. Where Radicals and Socialists were committed to political liberalism, communists preached the dictatorship of the proletariat. The leading role played by many communist activists in the wartime Resistance after Hitler's invasion of Russia enabled the PCF to drape itself in the French Tricolour as well as the Red Flag. After the war, it became the largest party on the Left, with over 25 per cent of the electorate, a strong trade union base, a mass membership and support from many intellectuals. For all its national role, however, the PCF's loyalty to the Soviet Union as the workers' homeland and to the principles of Marxism-Leninism remained intact.

The divisions within the French Left between its republican, socialist and communist families have not prevented periodic agreements, as in the 1936 Popular Front, to come together to 'defend the Republic' against its enemies. The myth of Left unity for the 'defence of the Republic' has been a powerful spur to electoral agreements right up to the 1980s. But there have always been plenty of enmities on the Left, based on ideological opposition and electoral rivalries. In the Fourth Republic, relations between the PCF and the SFIO were appalling and the latter collaborated in government with parties of the Centre Right (amongst which the Radicals were now numbered) to prevent the threat of a communist takeover.

The Right

Diversity on the Left is matched by diversity on the Right. The advent of parliamentary democracy did not lead in France, as it did in Great Britain, to the emergence of a dominant Conservative Party able to aggregate the beliefs and interests of social groups opposed to political and economic radicalism. Instead a variety of organisations sought to organise conservative politics. To explain this, the historian René Remond put forward the thesis, which has become very influential, of the existence in France of three conservative traditions: counter-revolutionary, parliamentary/Orleanist, and Bonapartist.

(a) *The Counter-revolutionary Right.*   Remond argues that sections of the French Right continued to oppose the principles of 1789 well into the twentieth century. Having been monarchist and clerical in the nineteenth century, the counter-revolutionary, or extreme, Right organised in quasi-fascist leagues in the 1930s and provided the ideological core of the anti-democratic and racist Vichy regime. The European-wide defeat of fascism destroyed the organisations of the extreme Right in France as elsewhere. But post-war problems of decolonisation and economic modernisation led to a revival in extreme Right activism in the 1950s under leaders like Pierre Poujade and Jean Marie Le Pen. The fact that Le Pen is now leader of the Front National shows, according to Remond, the durability of this 'counter-revolutionary' Right.

(b) *The Orleanist Right.*   The second of Remond's three groups is the parliamentary or Orleanist Right (the latter adjective referring to the family name of Louis Philippe, who was king of France between 1830–48). The parliamentary Right accepted constitutional government and, after 1875, the republican regime. Its liberalism was economic as well as political since it opposed collectivist welfarism, economic dirigism and redistributive taxation. The political parties of this Right were weakly organised before 1940 and they did not survive the Occupation and Liberation. In their place, an attempt was made to restructure moderate conservatism via the creation of a French version of the Christian Democracy that emerged elsewhere in western Europe. The Mouvement Républicain Populaire (MRP) aimed to be politically liberal, socially progressive, and European; it was also strongly anti-communist. An important party of government in the Fourth Republic whose ideas continue to influence sections of the present-day Right, the MRP saw itself as the voice of the political – and sociological – Centre. But, like earlier moderate parties, the MRP lacked a mass membership and a strong organisation, was prey to internal divisions and was challenged by more straightforwardly conservative parties like the Centre National des Indépendants et Paysans. In the Fifth Republic, the liberal Right has been represented by the UDF (see below).

(c) *The Bonapartist Right.* Remond defines the Bonapartist Right in terms of its dynamic view of the State, its nationalism, its cult of strong leadership and plebiscitary democracy, and its hostility to parliamentary government and parties. Since the Second World War, Gaullism has represented this tradition. In 1947 de Gaulle founded the Rassemblement pour la France as a leadership-based mass movement, pledged to the overthrow of the Fourth Republic and to the re-establishment of French *grandeur*. In the Fifth Republic Gaullism has been represented by a series of parties, or rather by the same party under a series of different names. It is currently known as the *Rassemblement pour la République.*

The notion of 'political families' helps us to understand the traditions and attitudes which provide ideological reference points, symbols and a vocabulary for parties. What it does not do is try to explain the choices made by parties and voters at any particular time. A present-day Gaullist no more responds to a given situation by asking what Napoleon would have done than a Socialist goes back to the writings of Jaurès to justify French membership of the European Monetary System. The existence

of political families did not, in the Fourth Republic, prevent all
the parties, save the Communists, from being internally divided
over major policy issues.

Parties in the Fifth Republic

The constitution of the Fifth Republic is the first in France's
history to refer to parties. It defines their role as competing
for the votes of universal suffrage and asserts their freedom
to organise and exercise their activity. Such constitutional
guarantees may seem paradoxical given de Gaulle's detestation
of parties. Yet the requirement that they respect the principles
of national sovereignty and democracy raised the spectre that those
who did not do so could be banned and the limitation of their
action to competing for votes hardly constituted a ringing assertion
of their place in the new order. The new constitution was, as
Chapter 2 shows, designed above all to weaken their influence.

With the exception of the Radicals (and to a lesser extent
the Communists), the political parties that had dominated the
Fourth Republic maintained their position in the first (1958)
elections of the Fifth Republic. Over the next twenty years,
however, the party system underwent major changes. The
fragmented, near anarchic multipartyism of pre-1958 politics
was replaced by disciplined coalitions on both Right and Left.
By the late 1970s the electoral politics of the Right was
dominated by two forces – the Gaullist *Rassemblement Pour
la République* and the Centre/Right *Union pour la Démocratie
Française* – neither of which had existed in 1958. On the
Left, the Communist and Socialist parties formed a union
on the Left which virtually monopolised the anti-conservative
vote. These two coalitions formed what became known as *the*
Majority and *the* Opposition, terms which had not really had any
meaning before. They aggregated almost the entire electorate
and contested elections at all levels, from the presidency to
the town hall; their electoral pacts were supplemented by
agreements on policy programmes.

It became very difficult for candidates to win if they did not have the support of the central organisations of one or other of the two coalitions, and rebellious deputies who broke with their party were usually defeated at the next election. The major parties took control of candidate selection in the constituencies and the number of round-two contests in which more than two candidates (one from each coalition) stood declined sharply. Small parties found themselves forced to throw in their lot with the big battalions of Majority or Opposition if they wished to maintain any parliamentary representation.

Bipolarisation is the ugly word used to describe the process whereby disciplined coalitions on Right and Left came to dominate French electoral and party politics. Bipolarisation is conventionally explained by reference to institutional and socio-cultural factors:

1. The two-round electoral system and the emergence of the directly elected presidency as the key political prize forced mainstream political parties to come together in coalitions if they were to have any chance of winning office. Power now flowed from the executive, incarnated by the President, rather than from the National Assembly and all the evidence suggests that the electorate liked it this way (see Chapter 2). Thus the new rules of the political game required parties who wanted to win to co-operate before and after – as well as during – election campaigns.

2. The changing contours of the electorate – more urban, more wage earning, more white collar, less churchgoing, less old – meant that the electorate was less fragmented sociologically, regionally and politically than it had been. Between 1959 and 1975 the percentage of the labour force employed in agriculture fell from 22 to 10 as over two million farmers left the land; the percentage of Catholics regularly attending mass declined from 37 in 1952 to 13 in 1981 (Flockton and Kofman 1989, pp. 47 and 72). At the same time 'modern' questions of how best to distribute the fruits of economic growth were replacing

the old questions of regime and religion as the focus of political debate. It has been argued that even before 1958 the old issues to which parties clung were of decreasing relevance to the voters. By emphasising the capacity of government to carry out long-term programmes, the Fifth Republic assisted the modernisation of political debate. The advent of mass television also helped to break down older political styles.

The division of the voters into two sociologically distinct camps did not come about overnight. De Gaulle's electoral appeal transcended class frontiers and in 1965 he polled strongly (42 per cent) amongst the manual working-class. (Frears, 1991 p. 143). But the vote of his two successors, Pompidou and Giscard d'Estaing, was increasingly concentrated in the non-wage earning categories. Giscard's narrow victory over his Socialist opponent Mitterrand in the 1974 presidential election – he won by 50.8 per cent of the vote to the latter's 49.2 per cent – demonstrated the reality of bipolarisation. Giscard's electorate was older, richer, more churchgoing and more highly educated than his opponent's. France's traditional electoral map had not been overturned; but electoral choice was being nationalised on socio-economic bases. At the same time the decline in church attendance meant that by the 1970s the Left, and particularly the Socialist Party, made gains in areas – notably Brittany and Alsace Lorraine – where it had historically been very weak.

The survival of multipartyism

The 1970s suggested that French electoral politics had come, as elsewhere, to be based on social class and the pursuit by two disciplined coalitions of governmental office. Yet the use of collective nouns like 'coalition', 'Majority' and 'Opposition' to describe party organisation indicates that multipartyism remained in place. Bipolarisation produced, as we shall see, new patterns of party organisation on both Right and Left. It did not, on the other hand, lead to 'two party' politics of the British or American sort. This in turn reflects the enduring relevance both of the political traditions described above and of the two-ballot system as a mechanism enabling parties within each camp to try to maximise their own identity.

The Right

In the 1960s, the Gaullist Party became the principal force on the Right. Under a variety of names (the Union pour la Nouvelle République, the Union des Démocrates pour la Cinquième République and the Union pour la Défense de la République), Gaullist candidates dominated conservative electoral politics. In the 1968 parliamentary elections, they obtained 37.3 per cent of the total vote and an absolute majority of seats in the National Assembly; the following year the Gaullist Pompidou easily won the presidential election that followed de Gaulle's resignation.

The Gaullist Party was tightly controlled by the government, support for which was its principal function. To avoid the risk of activists daring to try to influence the decisions of their leader, no attempt was at first made to attract a mass membership. Subsequently, a mass membership was sought, but there was no democratising of party decision-taking. Gaullism presented itself as a non-ideological (and non-clerical) force for the promotion of French *grandeur* via economic modernisation and political stability. Hostile to redistributive tax policies and to social liberalism, it was nevertheless unencumbered by rigid doctrinal positions. The party also acted as a recruiting agency for ambitious civil servants and business executives who wanted to enter politics.

Writing after de Gaulle's departure in 1969, Gaullism's most distinguished analyst, Jean Charlot, speculated that it might give France what it had always hitherto lacked – a British-type conservative party. He argued that its ability to survive the defeat of its founder, its pragmatism and national appeal made it the equivalent of modern 'catch all' right-wing parties elsewhere.

This was not to happen. Although the triumph of Gaullism in the 1962 parliamentary elections shattered the electoral positions of the extreme and centre Right parties that had opposed it, it did destroy other forms of conservatism. While the extreme Right disappeared as an electoral force, moderates and centrists sought to ensure their survival either by allying with the Gaullist Party or by organising for the time when de Gaulle had disappeared. The major Fourth Republic parties, the *Centre National des Indépendants et Paysans* and the *Mouvement Républicain Populaire* disintegrated. The former was succeeded by the Federation of Independent Republicans, founded by Giscard d'Estaing, which became the junior electoral and governmental partner of the Gaullists. The successor parties to the MRP tried to maintain the existence of the autonomous Centre as an independent force by putting up anti-Gaullist candidates in both parliamentary and presidential elections. Both Independent Republicans and Centrists emphasised their commitment to Europeanism and social reform, and offered the prospect of a less authoritarian style of presidential leadership.

Elections and events in the 1970s established a pattern of conservative party politics whose contours still (1993) exist. The presidential elections of 1974 confirmed what the 1973 parliamentary elections had suggested – viz that the Gaullist UDR did not exercise a hegemony over the conservative electorate. In the first round of the 1974 presidential contest, the Gaullist candidate, Jacques Chaban-Delmas obtained only 15 per cent of the vote compared with the 33 per cent that went to his rival Giscard d'Estaing. Chaban's failure to profit from the organisational superiority of the Gaullist Party shows the relative unimportance of party labels which was commented on earlier. By 1976 the UDR had not only lost the presidency but also the premiership. In the 1978 parliamentary elections, candidates of the RPR (as it was now called) won 22.6 per cent of the vote. Conservative victories in the 1974 and 1978 elections were the result of an electoral coalition between Gaullist and non-Gaullist parties that received the support of the increasingly homogenous conservative electorate (see above). In 1974 Giscard gained the support of the great bulk of Chaban's electorate as well as that of the centrist parties who had opposed de Gaulle. Four years later, the same coalition won a comfortable, if unexpected, victory in the parliamentary elections. Ministers from both camps participated in government throughout the Giscard presidency.

The ability of the parties of the Right to win elections together did not prevent a deterioration in their bilateral relations after 1974, which created a pattern of conflictual coalitionism that exists to this day (see Chapter 8). In part the conflict reflected Giscard's more progressive attitudes towards European integration and to social issues like abortion. But it also stemmed from the battle for political advantage between the Gaullists and the supporters of the new president. The former, under their ambitious new leader Chirac, aimed to re-establish their earlier pre-eminence among right-wing parties, and regrouped in the *Rassemblement pour la République*. Chirac was determined to make the RPR a vehicle for the maintenance of Gaullism's separate identity. Particularly after 1978, the RPR became a quasi opposition within the Majority. Its deputies were unwilling to provoke a constitutional crisis by overthrowing the president's government but its leadership did everything possible to weaken presidential authority.

Giscard and his allies were equally determined to prevent any return to the subordinate status they had possessed before 1974. Giscard linked together the various factions of the non-Gaullist Right and the Centre into a confederation known as the *Union pour la Démocratie Française* (UDF). The UDF had the status, and resources, that came from being the president's party; but the fact that it was composed of small, *cadre*-type parties meant that it lacked the mass membership of the RPR.

Political traditions of the sort identified by Remond played a role in the tensions between RPR and UDF and there is also evidence that after 1978 sections of the Gaullist electorate were less willing to accept Giscard. Yet the conflict between Gaullists and Giscardiens was essentially one between rival political elites battling for the right to represent the conservative electorate on round two of the presidential election. As such it shows another consequence of the effect of presidentialism on the party system.

The Left

The Fifth Republic posed a major challenge to the established parties of the Left. One reason for this was that dissatisfaction with the Fourth Republic record of the Socialist (SFIO) and Communist (PCF) parties led to the creation in the 1960s of a number of parties and political clubs which attempted to reshape the agenda of left-wing politics. Though a number of future Socialist leaders, including Rocard, came from these organisations, they failed to dislodge the existing parties. The real problem for the latter was that the new rules of the political game took power away from the National Assembly, the traditional locus of left-wing strength, and placed it in the presidency. Unless the new regime collapsed (which many desired but which became increasingly unlikely), the Left needed to come to terms with it. The problem was that Left traditions were hostile to *le pouvoir personnel* represented by the directly elected president and that 'the Left' was, as we saw above, a collection of strongly antagonistic parties.

Two strategies were advanced, both of which involved the construction of an electoral coalition broad enough to win the presidency. The first was the 1965 attempt by some SFIO and MRP leaders to create a coalition of the Centre and the Socialists, similar to those existing in the Fourth Republic and in many town councils, that would be at once anti-Gaullist and anti-communist. The attempt failed under the weight of traditional antagonism between clerical and anti-clerical parties. The second strategy involved trying to harness the five million Communist voters to an anti-Gaullist candidate of the Left. In 1965 François Mitterrand, then an independent anti-Gaullist, won the support of both Communist and Socialist parties for his self-declared candidature for the presidency. His unexpectedly good result – he won 44.5 per cent of the second round vote – had two lessons. It suggested that de Gaulle was not invulnerable and that a united Left could win the presidency.

Achievement of the electoral, and programmatic, co-operation necessary for the Left to win national power was far from easy. But the failure of Socialists and Communists to capitalise on the anti-Gaullist demonstrations of 1968 and the disaster of the 1969 presidential election, when all left-wing candidates were eliminated on the first round, were a powerful spur to unity. By 1970 it was obvious that the new institutional order based on a strong presidency was here to stay and that the only way for the Left to come to power was via the ballot box and inter-party co-operation.

In 1968–69 the SFIO drew the lessons of eleven years of political decay and refounded itself as the Parti Socialiste (PS). Shortly after, in 1971, it acquired a new leader, Mitterrand, who immediately worked to establish a programmatic alliance with the PCF (and with one fraction of the old Radical party), known as the Union of the Left. The alliance was based on a Common Programme of the Left whose symbolic importance lay in the PCF's acceptance of the principles of democratic elections and the PS's adoption of an economic policy inspired by neo-Marxist ideas of state planning and nationalisation. The alliance was the basis of the 1973 parliamentary election and of Mitterrand's candidature for the 1974 presidential campaign. Mitterrand was able to federate the entire Left electorate and won 49.2 per cent of the second round vote.

The year 1974 showed that a potential majority existed for a Socialist – but not for a Communist – presidential candidate. The new Parti Socialiste was a coalition of groups and traditions, united by opposition to the Right and by the prospect, for the first time in a generation, of winning governmental power. The party carried out a successful programme of organisational and policy modernisation. To an extent it took on the mantle of 'the new party for the new France' that the Gaullists had possessed in the 1960s. Whereas in the 1950s and

1960s the socialist electorate was ageing, and concentrated in traditional – and often economically declining – areas of strength, in the 1970s it now came to include the majority of the expanding numbers of under-30s (65 per cent in 1978) and of the salaried wage earners (65 per cent in 1978 as against 46 per cent in 1967). The membership base was middle class and managerial and resembled its SFIO predecessor in that it was strongly linked to the teaching profession: 47 per cent of the PS deputies elected in 1981 were teachers.

Presidential coalition-building was, however, just as likely to produce inter-party tensions on the Left as it had done on the Right. After 1974 the alliance of the Socialist and Communist parties known as the Union of the Left came under strain and in 1977 it broke down. The parties failed to renegotiate the Common Programme of Government; they entered the 1978 elections divided; and in the run-up to the 1981 presidential election were more antagonistic than at any time since 1958.

The split reflects the enduring ideological differences between French communism and French socialism referred to above. The 1972 Common Programme was written at a time of international detente and economic expansion. The economic difficulties (in particular unemployment) which followed the mid-1970s oil crisis put the policies of the Left into question. In 1977 the PCF demanded that the nationalisation programme be further strengthened, something which the Socialists and their Radical allies would not accept. Two years later, the PCF further radicalised – and isolated – its position by reverting to a position of unconditional pro-sovietism after the USSR's invasion of Afghanistan.

Disunion, however, had practical as well as ideological causes. For both Socialist and Communist parties, the goal of the alliance signed in 1972 was to maximise their own political strength. To this extent union was, as one communist leader said, a combat. By the mid-1970s, the Communist leadership realised that this combat was being won by the Socialist Party and that the five million votes the PCF polled were helping its rival to establish itself as the principal party of the Left. Only a socialist stood a chance of winning the presidency and the party had in François Mitterrand a leader of national and international stature. Increasingly, socialist candidates outpolled communists in parliamentary by-elections. The PCF feared that it would become a mere supplier of second-round votes to the PS and that the latter would thereby develop into the 'natural party of government' of the Left. This was something the PCF was not prepared to accept, since its influence within the political system resided in its ability to act as acknowledged spokesman for France's labouring classes.

In 1978, PCF determination to preserve its existing institutional and electoral bases took priority over the victory of a 'left' which it no longer dominated. By pulling out of the Left alliance and turning its fire on the PS, the PCF wanted to convince its own electorate that it alone could defend their interests, and to damage the PS pretensions to be a party of government. In the short term the strategy was successful. The Left unexpectedly lost the parliamentary elections and the prestige of the Socialist Party leader Mitterrand, the architect of the alliance strategy, was damaged.

Conflictual alliances and the 1981 elections

The apogee of conflictual bipolarisation was reached in the 1978 legislative elections when four parties of roughly equal strength (PCF, PS, RPR, UDF) divided the national vote equally between them (Cole 1990, p. 7). What was (untranslatably) called the *'quadrille bipolaire'* showed that no electoral space existed for parties outside it. Yet the antagonisms within each camp meant that the junior party within it (RPR on the Right, PCF on the Left) was ready to de-stabilise its coalition partner, even at the risk of provoking overall defeat.

For all the divisions on the Right, the Left's positions appeared more difficult thanks to the intransigence of the

PCF and the poor morale of the Socialist Party after the shock of 1978. Six months before the 1981 presidential elections, Giscard's re-election looked assured despite his growing unpopularity and the emergence of unemployment as the key issue. His eventual defeat at the hands of Mitterrand was thus a surprise.

As can be seen in Table 7.1, the first round of the election showed the voters' continuing attachment to the major parties. Despite their quarrels and the opportunity offered by the 'cost free' nature of the first-round vote to candidates coming from outside the coalitions, over 87 per cent of the voters opted for one of the four established parties. The second round, in which Giscard confronted Mitterrand was, as in 1974, the great simplifying duel between Left and Right that bipolarisation assumed. In the parliamentary elections that followed Mitterrand's victory, the parties in both coalitions presented a united front.

Yet the election also highlighted developments in the party system that the 1980s would accentuate (see Chapter 8).

On the Right, the failure of nearly 30 per cent of Chirac's RPR electorate to support Giscard on round two suggested a weakening in the solidity of 'system' conservatism, which the subsequent rise of the Front National confirmed. Chirac's virulent first-round attacks on Giscard and his very tepid endorsement of him for round two indicated that the leadership war between RPR and UDF was not going to go away.

On the Left, the election showed that the struggle for electoral advantage between Socialists and Communists had been decisively won by the former. A quarter of the PCF's existing vote defected on the first-round to Mitterrand. In part this reflects the sectarian strategy to which the party leadership returned after 1977. But it also reveals the emergence of a 'governmentalist' electorate on the Left, which preferred to vote usefully (i.e. for a candidate who can win), even when that candidate was not a PCF member. Mitterrand's victory, and the PS triumph in the legislative elections that followed in June, showed that the Socialists were now seen as the 'natural party of government' of the French Left. But it should be noted that Mitterrand won the presidency with just 26 per cent of the vote on round one of the presidential election and that the absolute majority the Socialist Party gained in the National Assembly derived from 38 per cent of the first-round vote. The result was a political earthquake, but it was not an electoral landslide.

Conclusion

There are two ways of looking at the impact of the Fifth Republic on parties.

Table 7.1 Presidential election 1981

	1st ballot		2nd ballot	
Electorate	36.4 million		36.4 million	
Abstentions	18.9%		14.1%	
Spoilt votes	1.4%		2.5%	
	million votes	%	million votes	%
Mitterrand (PS)	7.5	25.9	15.7	51.8
Marchais (PCF)	4.5	15.4		
Other Left	1.6	5.6		
Total Left	13.6	46.9		
Lalonde (Green)	1.1	3.9		
Giscard d'Estaing (UDF)	8.2	28.2	14.6	48.2
Chirac (RPR)	5.2	18.0		
Other Right	0.9	3.0		
Total Right	14.3	49.2		

Source: J. Frears, *Parties and Voters in France*. London: Hurst (1991, p. 157)

Anne Steven notes that by the 1980s a mechanism existed for the stable transfer of power from governments of one broad ideological persuasion to another (Stevens 1992, p. 221). This mechanism is provided by the parties and the presidential election. The four major political organisations – UDF and RPR on the one side, PCF and PS on the other – accepted the institutional framework of the Fifth Republic and, despite their internal rivalries, formed electoral and programmatic coalitions for the winning of governmental power. The large majority of the electorate cast their votes for candidates of these four parties not only in the 'high mass' moments of presidential contests but in the whole range of elections. The governmentalising of the Left meant that party politics now underpinned, rather than destabilised, the constitutional bases of power (see Chapter 2).

There is, however, another side to the story. The central role of the presidential contest has actually promoted, on both Left and Right, inter-party rivalry and intra-party fragmentation. In the run-up to the 1981 election, the leaderships of both the Communist and Gaullist parties were prepared to see their coalition partner lose the overall contest if it meant reinforcing their own position. Multipartyism, and the absence of mass party memberships, also make it very difficult to construct an American-style primary system. This means that potential presidential candidates will first attempt to get the backing of party elites, a process which encourages intra-party factionalism. Once recognised by the party, candidates must contest the real primary (round one) by emphasising the differences between them and their rival within the same camp. Should they win through to round two, they must then broaden their appeal by constructing an electoral and political union (rassemblement) that goes beyond their own party.

In their different ways, de Gaulle and Mitterrand were able to impose their authority on multipartyism and to transform electoral bipolarisation into disciplined party coalitionism. We shall see in the next chapter that in recent years multipartyism has become less disciplined and that problems of intra-coalition rivalry and party leadership have deepened. Perhaps, in consequence, the electorate has been less willing to support the two coalitions that have come to structure party politics in the Fifth Republic.

Further reading

John Frears, *Parties and Voters in France*. London: Hurst (1991).

8
Recent trends in party politics

Party systems have come under pressure in many western European states in recent years. The near collapse of the Italian system is the most extreme example, outside Eastern Europe, of the exhaustion of an existing form of party government. But in other countries, too, parties have been challenged by the emergence of new electoral attitudes and new issues. Examples of the latter include the rise of mass unemployment, the environment, immigration and the challenges to national sovereignty posed by European integration on the one hand and regionalist movements on the other.

Chapters 4 and 6 indicated some of the ways in which French policy assumptions have changed in the last ten years. The aim of this chapter is to describe and explain elements of continuity and change in France's electoral and party politics and to assess the current position and prospects of the parties.

Continuities

These are obvious. The single member, two-ballot voting system used for National Assembly elections (except in 1986) continues to help established parties and to distort electoral results despite the increase in the number of seats from 491 to 577. In 1981 the Socialist Party and its allies had won 58 per cent of the seats with 37 per cent of the first round vote; twelve years later the UDF/RPR coalition had 80 per cent of the seats, with 40 per cent of the round one vote. The Front National had no seats in the 1988 and 1993 National Assemblies despite gaining 10 per cent and 12.8 per cent of the vote respectively.

With the exception of the Communist Party, which has declined rapidly in the last ten years (see below), the three major groups – Parti Socialiste, Rassemblement pour la République, Union pour la Démocratie Française – continue to dominate the political landscape. All governments since 1981 have been controlled by them. Although a new cohort of politicians has emerged, often referred to as the 'forties generation' (*génération quadragénaire*), France's political personnel shows great continuity, certainly in comparison with Britain and the United States. Leading figures such as Mitterrand, Giscard d'Estaing, Chirac, Rocard and the Communist leader Marchais retain the central roles they have had since the early 1970s – and in some cases much earlier. (Mitterrand first entered Parliament in 1946 and Giscard in 1956). The most prominent 'newcomer' is Jean Marie Le Pen, who leads the Front National; he has been a professional politician since the early 1950s and, like Giscard, first became a deputy in 1956.

Despite the PCF's decline, the 'quadrille bipolaire' described in Chapter 7 still structures party alliances and each coalition is still racked by internal rivalries deriving from their struggle for pre-eminence. PS and PCF, RPR and UDF operate second-round electoral pacts and the latter co-ordinate first-round candidatures as well. The failure of the half-hearted attempt by prime minister Rocard in 1988 to realign the political bases of his parliamentary majority towards a Fourth Republic pattern of Centre-Left alliances shows the enduring nature of the Right–Left polarity. It confirms the fact that, although levels of party identification are lower than ever, the French continue to be able to identify themselves along the Left/Right continuum. The sociological characteristics of party electorates remain stable and voting is still determined by a mixture of social class and religious sentiment. Churchgoers are still more likely to vote for the Right, irrespective of social class.

French presidential, parliamentary and European elections continue to be fought by national parties on national issues. Regional, let alone separatist parties, have made no impact, not even in Corsica and there is no real equivalent to the Italian Lombard League or the nationalist parties of the United Kingdom. The political agenda is still shaped by the economic and social issues – particularly unemployment and law and order – that dominated the 1981 elections. Election campaigns are ever more dominated by national television and have become very expensive, so much so that laws now limit the amount candidates can spend on round one of the presidential contest (120 million francs (£15 million)) and on other contests.

For all the much talked about disaffection with politics, the French continue to be interested in politics and to vote often, and heavily. The year 1992 saw nationwide elections for regional councils in March and a referendum on the Maastricht Treaty in September. The National Assembly elections, held in March 1993, will be followed in 1994 by cantonal and European elections and in 1995 by municipal and presidential elections (unless Mitterrand resigns early). A 1991 SOFRES poll showed that between 1974 and 1991 the number expressing interest in politics rose from 54 per cent to 57 per cent. Though abstention rates have risen sharply for 'unimportant' elections (e.g. the 1988 referendum on New Caledonia), turn-out is high in elections regarded as important. Seventy per cent of registered voters turned out for the 1989 municipal, the 1992 regional and 1993 parliamentary elections. In 1988 84 per cent voted on the second round of the presidential contest, a figure that compares favourably with the United States experience.

Changes

1. The political agenda

Changes in the political agenda are of two kinds. On the one hand some important ideological baggage has been jettisoned by parties of both Right and Left, leading to claims that France now enjoys consensus politics. On the other, the new orthodoxies have themselves been challenged.

It was argued during the 1989 bicentennial of the French Revolution that two centuries of ideological civil war had finally ended and that France had finally entered upon its age of consensus, in which political activity took place within a shared set of assumptions about the organisation of political institutions and the role of government. The 1986–88 cohabitation period was taken as evidence of this. So too was the convergence over policy issues that resulted from two major parties – the RPR and the PS – carrying out big programmatic changes that led them to drop traditional economic objectives in favour of market-led, non-statist and anti-inflation policies (see below). Other elements of the consensus include the cross-party commitment to the 'strong franc' policy and membership of the EMS, and the widespread support given by the parties to French participation in the Gulf War. The PCF, which refused to rethink its ideology at a time when its historic role model – the Soviet Union – disintegrated and which opposed the Gulf War, has become much weaker.

The effect of the 'new consensus' should not be exaggerated. The tone of much French political debate remains very aggressive and prominent politicians, particularly in the Socialist Party, have been the victims of sustained, and highly personalised, vendettas by their opponents. Public faith in the honesty of politicians and parties is extremely low, a fact which explains the limits on campaign financing referred to above. More importantly, the consensus appears to have produced its opposite. The most spectacular, and controversial, political development since 1981 is the emergence of the far-right Front National as a significant electoral force. The Front National programme is based on the rejection of established political orthodoxies and as such challenges the convergences referred to above. The ideas espoused by the Front National, and articulated by its leader Jean Marie Le Pen, are not new; but after decades of public indifference they have begun to attract significant electoral support (see below). One consequence of this is that issues of immigration and race relations now have a much higher place on France's political agenda than was the case before 1981.

The breakthrough of the Front National is not the only change to have occurred in recent years. Ecology politics have also become more popular. The agenda of the Greens challenges major elements of the policy assumptions of the 1980s – nuclear power and the nuclear deterrent, the primacy of the motor car, French participation in the Gulf War and so on.

2. The decline in the hegemony of the two blocs

For all that the two coalitions remain in place, their capacity to control electoral choice is weaker than it was. In the 1993 legislative elections the four established parties won only 68 per cent of the first-round vote, compared with the 93 per cent they had gained in 1981. The share of the vote won by all the main parties is stagnant or falling. The national vote of the PCF has fallen by 50 per cent since 1981; more remarkably the PS gained only 17.5 per cent of the 1993 first-round vote compared with 37.5 per cent in 1981 and 34.7 per cent in 1988. The vote for the established parties of the Right is at best stable – its 'landslide' victory in the 1993 legislative elections was won with a smaller share of the vote than it polled in 1981 when it lost. The Maastricht referendum of September 1992 demonstrated the weakening hold of party leaderships over their electors. With the exception of the two 'outsiders' (PCF and Front National), the official line of all the major parties was to support the ratification of the Maastricht Treaty. Yet the referendum showed that 48.95 per cent of the voters opposed their leaders' support for the treaty.

Another sign of party weakness is deepening factionalism. All the parties have found it increasingly difficult to prevent the defeat of official candidates by rebels in local elections. Factionalism within parties has spread, as we shall see, from parties which always acknowledged the existence of internal factions (the PS and UDF) to the traditionally more authoritarian PCF and RPR. By 1990 it had run out of control in the Socialist Party.

Thus the four-party/two-bloc system of 1981 has been weakened as Table 8.1 shows. Six parties now have a significant electoral base, only two of which (RPR/UDF) are in formal alliance. The fact that both the Front National and the Ecologists stand outside the 1981 alliance system means that neither of the existing blocs can any longer claim to be *the* Majority. Two million voters spoiled their ballot papers on round two of the 1993 legislative elections – a remarkable figure.

Party performance

The Communist Left

In 1981 the PCF candidate for the presidency, George Marchais, obtained 15.1 per cent of the vote; seven years later, Andre Lajoinie won just 6.7 per cent. While it is true that presidential contests are particularly difficult for the PCF, in that it cannot hope to present a candidate capable of winning, it has failed to perform better in other elections. In the 1992 regional elections, for example, it won only 8 per cent of the

Table 8.1 Party share of the vote in the 1981 and 1993 National Assembly elections

Party	% share of the vote 1981	% share of the vote 1993
Parti Communiste Français (PCF)	16.1	9.14
Parti Socialiste (PS) and allies	37.8	19.24
Union pour la Démocratie Française (UDF)	19.2	18.84
Rassemblement pour la République (RPR)	20.9	19.69
Front National	1.3	12.69
Ecologists	–	10.92

vote, despite the collapse in the popularity of the PS, and in the 1993 National Assembly elections won fewer votes (2.7 million) than in 1988. (Its best 1993 result was in the Indian Ocean island of Réunion). In large parts of the country the PCF has ceased to exist as a political force. The remaining pockets of strength are in the working class areas of the Paris and Nord/Pas de Calais regions and in one or two rural areas; its overall national vote depends ever more heavily on areas where it still controls local government. The Communist electorate is masculine, poor and ageing – and very under-represented among women and young people.

Though the PCF held four posts in the Mauroy government appointed after Mitterrand's 1981 victory, it left office in 1984 and has no realistic prospect of returning. Nationally, its influence is restricted to the concessions that its parliamentary group was sometimes able to extract from the (minority) socialist governments in power from 1988–93. It continues to dominate the leadership of the CGT (Confédération Générale du Travail) union but this is a shadow of its former self with a membership of 500,000 (see Chapter 9). The prestige of the party amongst intellectuals has disappeared. Another sign of decline is the party leadership's loss of control over the Communist community in France. Throughout the 1980s oppositionist movements developed and in 1988 a dissident Communist, Pierre Juquin, stood for the presidency, winning 2.1 per cent of the vote. The current leadership is challenged from within by such figures as the Political Bureau member (and ex-minister) Charles Fiterman. Given that the defining characteristic of Communist organisation is the absolute authority of the party leadership, the existence of internal dissidence indicates the party's decay.

A number of reasons can be advanced to explain the Communist decline:

1. The party itself blames the Union of the Left strategy with the Socialist Party which operated between 1972 and 1977 and again from 1981 to 1984. It argues that by allowing

the Socialists to gain power, the PCF was no longer able to fulfil its historic mission of protecting working-class interests against the betrayals of social democratic government. The argument fails to explain why the party's decline continued, and accelerated, after the alliance ended and it reverted to a 'trade union' or 'tribune' role of defending the workers against the austerity policies of the Socialist governments of 1984–86 and 1988–93. A mere 11 per cent of manual workers voted Communist in the 1988 presidential election compared with 36 per cent who had done so in the 1978 legislatives. It is true that the presidentialising of electoral politics makes things difficult for parties that cannot win the key contest; but this has not prevented the rise of the Front National.

2. Changes in France's economic structure have led to a decline in the traditional industries – steel, shipbuilding, coal and so on – where a blue collar electorate provided the PCF with its electoral base. This is a problem that has affected other working class parties (cf. the Labour Party).

3. The collapse of the Soviet Union and the east European communist states, with which the PCF strongly identified, has shattered its claim to offer a better future than that offered by reformist capitalism. The PCF's commitment to Leninism and its unswerving support in the 1980s for the Stalinist regimes of eastern Europe did it great harm. More practically, the collapse of the USSR in 1991 deprived the party of important financial backing.

4. The party has suffered from poor, and ageing, leadership. The ideological rigidity of Marchais and his supporters and the authoritarian manner in which they respond to intra-party dissent have increased the party's isolation. Opinion polls regularly give very low ratings to Marchais and to the party he led until 1994.

The decline of French Communism has not brought any political dividends to the small, revolutionary factions of the extreme Left. Its function as a protest party – but not its electorate – has been taken over by the Front National.

The Socialist Party

During the 1980s the Socialist Party flourished. The party leader was president of the Republic and the party elite dominated government, except during the period of cohabitation. Possessing the status of the 'president's party' enjoyed by the Gaullists in the 1960s, its national appeal was consolidated. In the 1988 legislative elections it won over 30 per cent of the first round in all but one of France's twenty-two regions.

The sociology of its electorate showed it to be a 'catch all' party, well represented in most socio-economic groups and geographical regions (Bell and Criddle 1988, p. 197). In round one of the 1988 presidential election Mitterrand won 42 per cent of the manual worker – and 39 per cent of the white collar – vote; on round two he also for the first time in the history of the French Left gained a majority of the women's vote. The Socialist Party was the natural 'second-round' vote for the electorate of smaller parties like the Left Radicals, the Greens and the Communists and it had close links with anti-racist movements like SOS-Racisme (see Chapter 9).

The party changed its programme and elements of its belief system. The first two years of the Mitterrand presidency saw an ambitious programme of nationalisation and public spending to stimulate growth and an important series of social policy reforms. The failure of traditional left-wing economics led to a U-turn in 1983–84 and the adoption of market-orientated economic policies. French Socialists adopted the language of welfare capitalism, civil and social rights (the traditional concerns of Republicanism), anti-racism and Europe. In doing so they were helped by the collapse in the legitimacy of European Communism which allowed them to stop concealing their pragmatic reformism behind a rhetorical Marxism for fear of being outflanked on the Left. In opposition from 1986–88, the PS criticised the privatisation programme of the Chirac government, but they made no attempt to reverse the policy after Mitterrand's second victory in 1988 and indeed extended it (see Chapter 2). We have noted the break with the party's traditions in 1984 when Mitterrand abandoned its historical commitment to extending State control over church schools.

Thus by 1989 the Socialist Party had moved towards becoming a social democratic party of government. Its future looked assured. Yet today (1993) the party finds itself in severe difficulties. Party membership has slumped and the popularity of its leaders, in particular Mitterrand and his short-lived (1991–92) prime minister Edith Cresson, fell to levels never before seen in the Fifth Republic. The public image of the Socialists has been damaged by bitter factional disputes within the leadership over the issue of Mitterrand's succession and by a series of corruption scandals affecting prominent local and national figures. In late 1992, Laurent Fabius, the party general secretary (and Socialist prime minister from 1984–86) was almost impeached for his alleged role in a scandal involving the sale of AIDS-contaminated blood to hemophiliacs. Unable to bear charges of financial malpractice made against him, Pierre Bérégevoy, prime minister 1992–93, committed suicide shortly after the 1993 election.

The collapse in the reputation of the Socialist Party leadership has had dramatic electoral consequences. Between the 1988 and 1993 parliamentary elections the total vote for the Socialists and their allies fell from 9.1 million to 4.7 million. In the 1992 regional and departmental elections the party's share of the overall vote sank to under 20 per cent, and the image of the party was so negative that in some areas it relied on prominent non-Socialist personalities, like the controversial business tycoon Bernard Tapie, to head its candidate lists. A year later, in the more important parliamentary elections, the party did even worse. Not only did it fall back in the areas where it has made gains since the 1970s it also experienced unprecedented losses in its traditional heartlands in the north and south-west. Its earlier ability to appeal to second-round Green votes also waned.

A mixture of elements explain the present-day problems of the Socialist Party:

- The abandonment of much of the programmatic heritage of French Socialism – what Gaffney calls its ideological draining (Cole 1990, p. 81) – has left it without a clearly defined *project* that can mobilise committed support. Two of the three prime ministers between 1988 and 1993, Rocard and Bérégevoy, deliberately talked down programmatic ambition in the name of economic realities. Thus the PS became identified as a party of government, whose standing was heavily dependent on public assessment of government performance. Once Mitterrand and his ministers fell victim to sectoral discontents, rising unemployment, a series of scandals and voter fatigue (*usure*), party popularity fell. The decline of its reformist image was an important factor in its weakening appeal to supporters of minority parties like the Greens (79 per cent of whose voters had chosen Mitterrand in 1988 (Frears 1991, p. 163). It has also lost influence over immigrant pressure groups like SOS-Racisme.

- The Socialist *party* vote has always been smaller than Mitterrand's second-round vote suggested; in European and departmental elections the PS share of the vote is below 25 per cent. Mitterrand's second-round vote in 1988 was 3 million more than the total left-wing vote in round one, when he obtained 34 per cent of the vote. Thus the 1988 presidential majority is not a good guide to the core Socialist electorate since it includes some voters who did not vote for any of the six leftist candidates on round one.

- The party has suffered severe internal problems. Although the PS is formally a democratic party in which the National Congress is sovereign, it has a weak activist base and is effectively dominated by a number of powerful bosses (known as elephants) most of whom come from the parliamentary elite. Party membership is probably smaller than that of PCF and there is no trade union base. The party is composed of a number of *tendances*, (factions) which compete for members' votes in elections to its governing bodies. The *tendances* originally represented differing ideological traditions and derived their strength from a range of regional and institutional bases. In the 1970s this 'catch all' diversity had helped to broaden the electoral appeal of the Socialists and the party's leader, Mitterrand, was able to control the *tendances*. In the late 1980s, however, they increasingly became mere vehicles for the leadership ambitions of rival groups within the party elite, ambitions which Mitterrand was no longer able to control. The violence of intra-party factionalism, notably at the 1990 Rennes Congress, has caused great damage to the party's reputation and the undisguised hostility between Mitterrand and the party's leading figure, Michel Rocard, makes the choice of an acceptable successor difficult.

Thus it can seem as if presidentialism, having made the modern Socialist party, is now unmaking it. The struggle between rival factions for the party's nomination as presidential candidate has harmed its reputation for political integrity and the loss of a clear reformist identity has made it dangerously dependent on its record in government. Popular rejection of that record inevitably led to the 1993 electoral disaster.

There is however another side to the story. The Socialists are now experiencing the same problems of over-exposure to power that affected the Gaullist UDR in the early 1970s and led to its vote falling from 37 per cent in 1968 to 15 per cent in 1974. Party Gaullism survived the defeat of 1974 and it is difficult to envisage the PS failing to do the same. It has a number of potential presidential candidates, notably Rocard and the current (1993) president of the European Commission Jacques Delors, and a strong base in the town halls. It is also the only party with broad appeal to wage earners in the public and private sector. The party's immediate, and linked, tasks are to distance itself from the unpopularity of Mitterrand and his governments, to overcome the factionalism of the last few years and to construct a new reformist identity. It faces a difficult electoral calendar in that the next presidential election is only two years away (1995). The biggest challenge, however, lies in constructing an electoral coalition that can replace the shrunken union of the Left. The last decade has shown its inability to transform the potential second-round vote for a Socialist presidential candidate into an 'all election' vote.

The ecology parties

The emergence of Green politics in France reflects both a Europe-wide concern with environmental issues and the impact of the 1968 events in France in mobilising a core of activists against the excesses of industrial society. Since the early 1970s Green groups have taken advantage of the opportunities provided by national elections – presidential and European – to mobilise support for their cause. In the first round of the presidential elections of 1974, 1981 and 1988 Green candidates won 1.4 per cent, 3.7 per cent and 3.8 per cent of the vote respectively and they did even better in the 1979, 1984 and 1989 elections for the European Parliament with 4.5 per cent, 6.7 per cent and 10.8 per cent of the vote. The latter result gave them 10 MEPs in a year in which they also won 1400 town council seats. In 1992 Green candidates obtained 14.7 per cent of votes and gained representation in most of the regional councils.

Thus there is a Green sensibility in France which is nurtured by the frequency of elections. It has not, however, been easy to organise Green politics into a unified force. As elsewhere (Britain and Germany), a basic split exists between radical ecologists and reformist environmentalists. More specifically French are the absence of a large activist base and the issue of Green relations with established parties. The majority of activists belong to Les Verts, the 'green' political party founded in 1984 with Antoine Waechter as a spokesman (the notion of leader is rejected). Les Verts (the Greens) reject the established coalitions of both Right and Left on the grounds that they are equally wedded to anti-environment models of economic growth. But there is another group, Génération Ecologie, which is more sympathetic to alliances with the democratic Left. Its leader, Brice Lalonde, was Minister of the Environment in the post-1988, socialist governments and received financial help for his candidates from pro-government sources in the 1992 regional elections.

In 1993, the two Green parties overcame their suspicion of each other, and of the parliamentary game, to form a nationwide electoral alliance. But they did much worse than predicted, obtaining only 7 per cent of the votes compared with poll estimates of 15 per cent. All but two of their candidates were eliminated on round one and they failed to elect a single deputy. The result showed, once again, that the performance of 'cause' parties depends on the nature of the election and that they have difficulty in presenting a credible programme for contests that affect the overall shape of government. It also confirmed that the Green electorate does not always turn pink on round two.

The Right

Overall electoral statistics for the Right tell a story of recovery after the 1981 defeat. In the 1983 municipal elections, Conservative parties regained an overall plurality of the national vote which they have never subsequently lost. In 1986 the three conservative parties – RPR, UDF, FN – won 54.7 per cent of the total and in 1988 they had 50.9 per cent of the first-round vote in the presidential elections. In 1993 the Right won 56 per cent of the total first-round vote.

Yet the obvious point to make about this arithmetic electoral lead is that, except in 1986–88 and since March 1993, it has not been translated into the winning of national office. Moreover, in the second round of the 1988 presidential election Jacques Chirac, the Right's standard-bearer, won only 46 per cent of the vote. This situation is conventionally explained by reference to two linked factors:

1. The existing parties – RPR and UDF – have failed to put

an end to the rivalries that contributed to their defeat in the 1981 presidential campaign. No leader has yet emerged in either group capable of dominating the leadership of the Right and appealing to the sum of its electorates in the election that matters most – the presidency.

2. The rise of the anti-system Front National has cost the parties of the established, or 'respectable' Right their ability to monopolise the non-Left electorate. An 'extreme' as well as a 'system' or 'republican' Right now exists which for the first time in the Fifth Republic is strong enough to influence the political prospects of the latter.

Analysis of the Right needs to take account of both these developments. The rise of the Front National has posed problems of policy and strategy for the 'system' Right – and divisions over the appropriate response have exacerbated tensions within, and between, the UDF and RPR.

The System Right: Rassemblement pour la République and Union pour la Démocratie Française

Chapter 7 showed that the RPR and UDF represent differing political and organisational traditions within French conservatism. The RPR claims a mass membership and has a top-down leadership style, the UDF is a more decentralised cartel that brings together the leaders of a number of smaller parties of which the most important are the Parti Republicain and the Centre des Démocrates Sociaux.

Over the last decade some of the differences separating the two groups have weakened, mainly as a result of policy shifts within the RPR. In the early 1980s, the RPR adopted the market liberalism and pro-Europeanism about which it had hitherto been ambiguous. The old Gaullist belief in an economically interventionist State and in a strong public sector has been tempered by the commitment to market forces and privatisation articulated by newer leaders like Edouard Balladur (finance minister 1986–88, prime minister 1993–). Chirac's acceptance as prime minister between 1986–88 of the Single European Act and an extensive programme of selling off nationalised industries marked a break with the traditions of Gaullism that brought it closer to UDF.

This policy evolution has helped the RPR and UDF to present a common programme of government in 1986 and in 1993 and to work harmoniously in government at both national and local level. An umbrella organisation, the *Union pour la France*, was founded after 1988 to promote unity and electoral co-operation and the latter, at any rate, has been good. In the 1993 parliamentary elections, for example, there were only 65 official first-round primaries between candidates of the two groups. There is a double reason for this. Each party has well-defined geographical areas of strength on which the other does not lightly poach. The RPR has held on to the strongholds it possessed in 1981 (right-wing departments in western France and two areas – the Limousin region and Paris and its affluent suburbs – where Chirac's influence is very strong). The UDF does well in the south and in traditionally Catholic areas in western and eastern France. Secondly, the bulk of the conservative electorate finds it easy to vote for either party on round two despite some sociological differences between RPR and UDF voters. Both parties find it difficult to win votes from blue collar workers and from public sector employees.

For all these convergences, the separate identity remains in place. Sections of the UDF, and in particular the Christian Democratic-based Centre des Démocrates Sociaux, are uneasy with the muscular authoritarianism that characterises the RPR attitude to law and order and race issues and with the aggressiveness of Chirac's leadership style. These anxieties found expression in the campaign of Raymond Barre, the UDF candidate in the 1988 presidential election; a fifth of Barre's round-one vote in 1988 declined to support Chirac on round two. More important, the deep-seated rivalry between Chirac and Giscard d'Estaing continues to empoison relations between the two parties as each battles to establish itself as the 'natural' leader of the Right. The continuing absence of a 'primary' mechanism for the selection of a conservative candidate for the presidency means that intra-coalition tensions fester. After the 1993 parliamentary election, the RPR prime minister Balladur took great care to appoint prominent UDF figures, in particular from the CDS, to his government, in order to maximise inter-party harmony. It was, however, immediately clear that the UDF president, Giscard d'Estaing, would not accept RPR hegemony over the new Majority.

The 1988 defeat also produced new tensions *within* each of the parties as questions of policy merged with battles over leadership. Inside the UDF, the Centre des Démocrates Sociaux formed a separate independent parliamentary group as a way of indicating their programmatic independence and ran a separate list in the 1989 European elections. Giscard's authority as leader of the UDF has been challenged by younger leaders like François Léotard. In 1992 a prominent Republican Party figure Philippe de Villiers formed a new movement, Combat for Values (Combat pour les Valeurs), which challenged the Europeanism and social liberalism with which the UDF leadership is identified.

Although respect for the leader is a part of the culture (if not always the practice) of Gaullism, its leader Chirac also came under fire from inside his party. In 1981 two dissident Gaullist candidates had made minimal impact on RPR electors and activists. But after 1988 a number of younger Gaullist mayors of big cities (Noir at Lyons, Carignon at Grenoble) complained about the outdatedness of the party's profile. More seriously, Charles Pasqua, a right-wing heavyweight and close adviser of Chirac (whose Minister of the Interior he was between 1986–88), joined with one of the party's leading younger figures Philippe Seguin in demanding that the RPR abandon its neo-liberalism for a more authentically 'Gaullist' policy of economic interventionism, social reform and opposition to moves towards European integration. Unlike earlier critics of Chirac's leadership, Pasqua and Seguin succeeded in establishing a strong base amongst RPR activists and in 1992 put themselves at the head of RPR opposition to ratification of the Maastricht Treaty which Chirac supported (see Chapter 10).

The success of the *Union pour la France* in 1993 led to the formation of the Balladur government in which, as we have seen, all sections of the alliance are represented. The overwhelming parliamentary majority – the UPF has 80 per cent of the seats compared with 51 per cent in 1986 – and the weakness of the Socialists provides a strong basis for the 1995 presidential election. But candidacy and policy (Europe) questions remain. So too does the challenge presented by the emergence of the radical, or rogue, Right of the Front National.

The challenge of the Front National

Chapter 7 noted the existence of a 'radical' Right tradition in France that survived the European-wide discrediting of fascism in the Second World War. In the Fifth Republic a combination of socio-cultural and institutional factors – the end of Empire, de Gaulle's new nationalism, economic prosperity, bipolarisation – destroyed the electoral bases of right-wing extremism. Right-wing activism survived, but had negligible political, and no electoral, effect. The Front National, founded by Jean Marie Le Pen in 1972, had no success in the elections of the 1970s – and in 1981 Le Pen was unable to find the 500 signatures of local councillors necessary for him to stand in the presidential election.

Yet in the early 1980s the extreme Right emerged from the political wilderness it had inhabited since the loss of French Algeria. Through its leader, the Front National became the champion of a 'France first' policy that blamed economic and social difficulties on immigration, and in particular on the many North African families that had settled in France, with the simple equation 'two million unemployed equals two million immigrants too many'. Le Pen demanded the exclusion of immigrant families and an end to the social security benefits to which they were entitled. He also made violent attacks on the permissive society, demanding the compulsory isolation of

AIDS victims, the reintroduction of the death penalty and an end to legalised abortion. The Front National opposes all moves towards closer European integration and the Brussels bureaucracy as a threat to national identity. It also condemns the existing political elite of other parties – right as well as left – for being corrupt and bankrupt.

The Front National programme represents an assault on the conventions, and on the leaders, of conservative politics in the Fifth Republic. Although commentators disagree over the extent to which Le Pen's programme is fascist, its most dedicated activists come from the anti-republican Right – the supporters of Marshal Pétain's Vichy regime, French Algeria, reactionary Catholicism and, in some cases, the Monarchy. But the Front has also attracted a number of top civil servants, business executives and right-wing intellectuals. Le Pen himself has a long history of involvement in neo-fascist organisations and is an admirer of the Italian fascist party, the MSI. His racism does not stop at the new immigrant communities in France and extends to a deep seated, and imperfectly concealed, anti-semitism. The latter lies behind his opposition to French involvement in the United Nations coalition against Saddam Hussein at the time of the Gulf War.

If the traditions to which the Front National appeals are long established, its electoral success is new. Three years after the 1981 debacle, it gained 11 per cent of the votes cast in the European elections. Voting in the latter is, of course, 'cost free' to the extent that the election does not have any impact on domestic policy. But the Front then went on to score 10 per cent in the parliamentary elections of 1986 and 1988. In the 1988 presidential election, Le Pen polled 4.4 million votes – 14.4 per cent of the total – and in 1993 Front National candidates won 12.7 per cent of the first-round poll. This durability of the Front's electoral appeal is among its most significant characteristics. Unlike other 'flash' parties, it has not faded away after an initial success and now appears to have established itself firmly in certain regions and social groups.

How should the Front National's success be explained? It does not derive from widespread nostalgia for the Vichy regime or for fascism, despite the fact that some of its activists and on occasions, when he is sufficiently roused, Le Pen himself, manifest their hostility to the humanist values associated with liberal democracy. Nor is it solely due to Le Pen's considerable abilities as public speaker and television performer. Mitterrand's decision to introduce proportional representation for the 1986 National Assembly elections helped (and was unquestionably intended to help) the Front National to establish itself at the expense of the RPR and UDF. But the party has more than survived the return to a two-round voting system designed to penalise extreme parties and has profited, in a way that the Communist Party has not, from a presidential contest which it cannot hope to win.

To understand the Front's success we thus need to look at the political context of the 1980s. The failure of the Socialist government to increase employment and reduce inflation led to public opinion in France (as in other liberal democracies) moving sharply away from the Left. The agenda of politics shifted from reform to security. The difference between France and the United States and Britain was that the established conservative parties were unable to control the sense of frustration and anxiety with policy failure. Le Pen taps the 'anti-party' vein in French politics which we have noted several times before by claiming to speak for the 'ordinary' French people over the heads of the political class. It is a style of politics which identifies scapegoats and makes them the cause of problems. Polls taken at the 1988 presidential election showed that the three principal themes motivating Le Pen's electorate were immigration (59 per cent), insecurity (55 per cent) and unemployment (41 per cent). Significantly, many of those who voted for Le Pen did not expect or even want him to be elected president.

The geographical implantation of the Front National differs from traditional areas of right-wing strength, although it is not, as is sometimes suggested, the successor party to the

Communists. Its electoral heartland lies in the departments
of the deep south – Alpes Maritimes, Bouches du Rhône,
Gard, Hérault, Pyrenées Orientales, Vaucluse, Var – where the
legacy of French Algeria is strong. It also does well in declining
industrial areas in the north and north-east and in the decaying
outer suburbs of big cities (Paris, Lyons) in which immigrant
communities are concentrated. The vote is thus an 'inter-class'
response to the problems of the urban society constructed in the
1960s and to the difficulties facing traditional economic sectors
which European integration exacerbates. In 1988 Le Pen
gained a greater share of the unemployed vote than did the
PCF candidate and more workers than either the RPR or
UDF candidates. His electorate is predominantly masculine
and composed in the main of self-employed groups (farmers,
artisans, shopkeepers), employees and workers.

The reason why the Front National has attracted such
attention is that, in placing immigration at the heart of the
political agenda and in the tone of its political rhetoric, it
has revived anxieties about France's past record, and future
prospects, as a liberal democracy. Its principal impact, however,
lies in the problems of principle and of strategy which it poses
to the parties of the system Right. They cannot adopt its credo
without betraying the universalistic values of French republican
democracy and alienating their more moderate voters. But total
condemnation of the themes raised by Le Pen risks the loss
of their own supporters and activists; the RPR in particular
is vulnerable to the fact that Le Pen has been able to set the
agenda for conservative politics. Thus the RPR and UDF have
been divided in their response. Some leaders have refused any
compromise with Front National themes while others, including
Chirac and Giscard d'Estaing have given not-so-coded support
to its racism by adopting some of its imagery. In 1988 Mitterrand
used the spectre of Chirac's compromise with Front National
themes as part of his 'republican' message designed to appeal
beyond the Left.

The strategic dilemma follows from the above and can be
easily summarised:

- So long as the Front polls 10 per cent of the vote, the Right cannot win the presidency unless the bulk of its electorate transfers on round two. In 1988 only about 60 per cent of them did so.
- The Right will not win the presidency if centrist voters believe it has yielded to the Front National's conditions for an electoral pact.

The situation is not dissimilar to that which used to face the democratic Left in its relations with the PCF: how to acquire the votes of a party which is perceived to be extreme without losing overall electability. Le Pen has tried to coerce the Right into compromise by telling his supporters not to vote on round two for the moderate Right. In 1988, 35 per cent of them followed his advice. One question for the future is whether Front electors will continue to follow their leader's advice to sabotage the established Right's chances. Another is whether the Front will maintain its share of the vote with – or without – Le Pen. Like other parties, the Front National too has experienced conflicts and resignations; but Le Pen's appeal to the grass-roots remains for the moment intact.

Conclusion

The balance sheet of French parties is mixed. They are less able than ever to attract a mass membership and public apathy towards them has shown signs of deepening into antipathy. The electoral hegemony of the two coalitions of Right and Left has declined and parties in government have failed to reduce what the electorate consistently regards as the most important policy issue, unemployment. On the other hand, the party system constructed in the 1960s and 1970s still determines the decisive electoral contests of presidency and National Assembly and still supplies the personnel of government. The French party system may be under strain; but it is premature to talk of a generalised crisis of political representation.

Further reading

D. S. Bell and Byron Criddle, *The French Socialist Party*. Oxford: Clarendon Press (1988).

Alistair Cole (ed.), *French Political Parties in Transition*. Aldershot: Dartmouth (1990).

9
Pressure groups

The conventional view of pressure groups in France is that they are weak. Compared with other industrialised democracies like Britain, Germany and Sweden, France is seen to lack well-established cause and interest groups, whose influence derives from their ability to recruit widely in the sphere they represent and from the power – and the legitimacy – that this gives them in their dealings with government and employers. According to this view, neither pluralism – multiple groups competing on equal terms for influence in the political market-place – nor neo-corporatism – shared decision-taking by government and producer groups – really exist in France.

Explanations for the supposed weakness of organised groups include:

1. the individualism of the French, who simply do not like joining organisations;
2. the chronically fragmented nature of existing interests which are all too often divided on ideological or status lines;
3. the authoritarian nature of public authorities, particularly in the Fifth Republic, and the absence of a pluralist culture.

The assertion that ever since the French Revolution the State has been unwilling to acknowledge the legitimacy of interest groups, regarding them as potentially subversive of national unity, should by now be familiar. It is significant that the often used, and pejorative, term *féodalités* (feudalities) used to describe interest groups equates them with the power structures of pre-democratic France. This equation of pluralism with group selfishness was a particularly marked characteristic of Gaullist rhetoric; but it does not date from the Fifth Republic and it is certainly not limited to one particular party. In the past, parties of the far Left and Right denounced the occult power of the so-called 'two hundred families' (the leading business groups) and other targets included the Jesuits, the Freemasons and the Jews.

The conventional picture of a powerless, atomised society passively, if resentfully, accepting the commands of an authoritarian State is, however, much over-simplified. The weakness of institutionalised interest groups does not mean that France is immune to outbreaks of sectoral pressure or that elected governments and business leaders are able to ignore it. Anyone caught up in the lorry drivers' dispute that paralysed the country's road network in early July 1992 will know just how ruthless a determined interest group can be in France. The ability of French farmers to engage in direct action of varying degrees of violence is legendary. So too is its immediate consequence, which is the difficulty of revising the Common Agricultural Policy of the European Community and the GATT arrangements for international trade. Nor is direct action the monopoly of farmers. In recent years there have been prolonged strikes involving postal and railway workers, air traffic controllers, health workers, prison officers and teachers.

The symbolic violence that often accompanies pressure group action in France derives from the weakness of organised pluralism – protesters have nowhere to go other than on to the streets – and from long-established, almost theatrical patterns of public protest. Such forms of protest may be very effective in their prime purpose of winning concessions from government. They do not represent – as overseas commentators are prone to believe – a revolutionary assault on the legitimacy of the regime. The most famous demonstrations in the post-war history of western Europe – the French 'events' of May 1968

– were not, as was widely claimed at the time, a revolutionary challenge to capitalist society and State; but they did succeed in unblocking the political situation (de Gaulle resigned within a year) and they did produce important improvements in social benefits and trade union rights.

Elsewhere on the socio-economic scale the ability of sectoral interests in France to entrench their privileges is real enough. The highly organised caring professions have made reform of the health and education (and prison) systems very difficult and French schoolchildren and students are much more successful than their British counterparts in stopping educational changes of which they disapprove. Business, big and small, can be very effective in obtaining its sectoral goals, be it small shopkeepers seeking to control the granting of permits to supermarkets or large companies forming close links with government departments. An example of the former occurred in 1993 when the newly-elected Balladur government, supposedly committed to market forces, drew up measures to protect small rural commerce from the spread of hypermarkets. As regards the latter, Jolyon Howorth has referred to the ability of what he calls the 'military-industrial complex' in 1987 to get government to approve a new fighter plane in defiance of both military and political advice (Hall, Hayward, Machin 1990, p. 210).

The study of pressure group activity in France thus needs to distinguish between different types of pressure groups and to assess their differing resources, strategies and points of access to policy makers.

Cause groups

Cause groups concerned with value goals like the preservation of wildlife and the national heritage are comparatively weak in France. It is difficult to find a French equivalent for mass membership groups like the National Trust or the Royal Society for the Protection of Animals. That this should be so reflects national value attitudes. Anne Stevens has convincingly suggested that the relative weakness of the numerous environmental pressure groups may reflect continuing popular identification with the economic interests of the peasant and the leisure pursuits of the hunter – two categories that hardly exist in older industrial societies – rather than a national refusal to participate in group activities. Distinct perceptions of the French national interest also help to explain why the Campaign for Nuclear Disarmament has never had the support in France that it did elsewhere (see Chapter 10) – and why Corsica has a number of banned independence movements that use bombs and guns to promote their cause.

Although published statistics suggest that 46 per cent of the population belong to at least one association, Hollifield argues that 'citizen politics' is relatively weak in France compared with other post-industrial societies (Hollifield and Ross 1991, p. 281). He attributes this to the persistence of republican and nationalist ideals which provide a uniquely French model of political participation and citizenship.

Yet in some 'cause' areas – education and the family – strong pressure groups do exist. Part of their salience is due to the fact that they are identified with one of the two sides in the continuing debate (and struggle) between Catholics and non-Catholics over the control of education, a debate that affects the content of public policy. The *Fédération des Conseils de Parents d'Elèves* groups 650,000 families in state schools and the *Union Nationale des Associations de Parents d'Elèves de l'Enseignement Libre* groups 860,000 families associated with the Catholic schools. The power of the latter was shown in its ability in 1984 to mobilise hundreds of thousands of demonstrators in a (successful) protest against the education reforms of the Socialist education minister Alain Savary. In the past, and to some extent today, Freemasonry has been seen as exercising influence over the parties of the non-communist Left.

The link between pressure group success and the broader political environment is shown by the rise of one of the most successful cause groups of recent years SOS-Racisme, founded in 1985 to counteract the growing influence of Le Pen's National Front. Under its leader Harlem Désir, SOS-Racisme has attracted a large membership and ran a highly successful pro-integration campaign with the theme 'leave my pal alone' ('Touche pas à mon pote'). The movement received moral and financial support from the Socialist government (in 1992 for example Jack Lang's Culture Ministry gave 1.800000 francs – £200,000 – for its annual 14 July festival). Another effective pressure group leader is the Abbé Pierre, who campaigns for the homeless and was able in July 1992 to embarrass the public authorities into providing accommodation for destitute immigrant families. In the aftermath to 1968, a strong, if divided, feminist movement emerged that was effective in raising the consciousness of a notoriously male-dominated political class to women's issues and led to liberalised divorce and abortion laws.

Interest groups

In industrial democracies, the most prominent interest groups are those organised in both the private and public sectors by labour and employers. No account of post-war British politics and society would be complete without reference to the umbrella producer group organisations of the Trade Union Congress and the Confederation of British Industry and to the organisations that affiliate to them. Even today, after thirteen years of anti-trade union government and the abolition of the National Economic Development Council as a forum for permanent discussion between government and the two sides of industry, 40 per cent of the British work-force is unionised. The situation in France is different.

Workers and farmers

Levels of trade union membership in France have always been very low compared with other industrialised countries. Only about 25 per cent of the work-force was unionised in the early 1970s and today the figure is an astonishingly small 10 per cent. Large sectors of private industry are virtually un-unionised. The number of days lost through strikes fell by half between 1973 and 1982.

At national level five trade union confederations compete for such union membership as there is – *Confédération Générale du Travail, Confédération Française et Démocratique du Travail, Force Ouvrière, Confédération Française des Travailleurs Chrétiens, Confédération Générale des Cadres.* In elections for workplace committees, the CGT gets about 20 per cent of the vote followed by the CFDT (11 per cent) and FO (10 per cent). Membership of the CGT, historically France's largest union, is now down to about half a million.

The fragmented nature of trade unionism does much to explain the low level of membership. Only rarely does a single union have the clout that comes from being able to speak for all the workers in a given industry; hence there is little practical incentive for an employer to negotiate or for an individual worker to take out a union card. French employers have in any case always been very reluctant to acknowledge the bargaining rights of trade unions, particularly over pay. The relative weakness of unions' industrial muscle means that trade union activity in France has been primarily aimed at influencing the political parties of the Left since it is only through the State, and through legislation, that its interests can be advanced (see below).

Trade union divisions reflect its high level of politicisation. This is a state of affairs that sits uneasily with the labour movement's founding 'statement of intent', the 1906 Amiens Charter which proclaimed French trade unionism's independence of any political party. There was to be no equivalent in France of the union–party linkages that created British Labourism. French trade union dues do not include a political levy. Politics is nevertheless crucial to understanding French trade unionism. The key factor in its post-war history is the control of the largest confederation, the CGT, by the

Communist Party. The new general secretary of the CGT, Louis Viannet, is a member of the PCF political bureau, as were all his post-war predecessors. The CGT's regional and industrial organisers are nearly all communist activists, although most ordinary members are not. Despite its self-proclaimed independence from party politics, the CGT endorsed the Communist candidates in the presidential contests of 1981 and 1988 and throws its organisational power behind the party in all electoral campaigns. The CGT leadership views industrial relations in terms of the class struggle and defines its role in Leninist terms as being an agent of the Communist Party. It is prepared to reach deals with public and private sector employers but resolutely rejects anything that smacks of consensual – let alone neo-corporatist – styles of bargaining or of the acceptance of the political economy of capitalism.

Trade unionists who reject communist dominance of organised labour have thus had no alternative to forming separate organisations. Force Ouvrière (FO) was founded in 1948 out of Cold War–inspired conflicts between communist and non-communist groups within the CGT, and the Confédération Française et Démocratique du Travail came into being in 1964 as a result of a schism within the Catholic-based CFTC. Both Force Ouvrière and the CFDT proclaim their political independence and their purely trade union vocation – but both are inevitably suspicious of communist labour strategies. They were prepared in the 1970s to engage in joint action with the CGT but once the political alliance between PCF and the PS broke down in 1977 (see Chapter 7) this stopped. Particularly in the 1970s, the CFDT had close, albeit informal, links with the Socialist Party. The traditionally deal-minded FO has under a new leader, Marc Blondel, become more militant in its dealings with government and employers.

Some public sector professions remain highly unionised. Until recently the various sections of the teaching profession were organised into the Fédération de l'Education Nationale (FEN), an umbrella organisation that linked the elementary (SNI) and secondary (SNES) teachers' unions and exercises considerable, usually blocking, influence over education policy, especially when Socialists are in power. The reason why in 1984 the Mauroy government was unable to impose its legislation on the organisation of Church schools was that many of its parliamentary supporters were ex-teachers with close links to the FEN. They barred the compromise worked out between the education minister Savary and the Church authorities – whose own pressure groups then promptly organised massive protests. Yet here again conflict between communists and non-communists persists and the FEN has recently broken up.

The visibility (and audibility) of farming organisations has already been noted and was demonstrated in September 1991 when 300,000 farmers marched through Paris. The largest farming union is the Fédération Nationale des Syndicats d'Exploitants Agricoles, which groups about half of French farmers and has considerable influence on the Ministry of Agriculture, and on the RPR. Its leader, François Guillaume, was minister of agriculture in the 1986 Chirac government. Another influential farming pressure group is the Centre National des Jeunes Agriculteurs which is in regular contact with government officials. As with labour organisations, the farming community is divided. In 1988 the Confédération Paysanne was founded to fight for the interests of small farmers. Its members have been responsible for the violent demonstrations that periodically shatter the apparent tranquillity of the French countryside and make it dangerous, and sometimes impossible, for government ministers to travel outside Paris.

Business and the professions

The peak-level business organisation is the Conseil National du Patronat Français. As an umbrella organisation linking about 800 widely differing trade associations it has little power over affiliates like the engineering employers' Union des Industries Métallurgiques et Minières. It is also perceived to be the spokesperson of big business, despite the fact that one of its members is the small business union, the

Confédération Générale des Petites et Moyennes Entreprises. France also has a long history of aggressive unionism by organisations pledged to defend the small man against the incursions of big business and big government. Organisations like the small shopkeepers' CID-UNATI and the present-day Syndicat National des Petites et Moyennes Industries share the capacity of their farming equivalents to be rude to government ministers. Their aggressiveness is, however, a result of their economic weakness. Other sectoral groups have less need to go into the streets to maintain their advantages. The French author François de Closets has written a number of bestselling accounts, the most famous of which is 'Toujours Plus' (1987), of the employment and economic privileges enjoyed by particular groups from bankers to full-time staff on the Paris underground. Middle class professions like architects and pharmacists are able to operate an effective closed shop. In recent years, the American concept of lobbying has gained wide currency and in 1991 a professional organisation of *lobbymen* was created by a number of companies which specialise in this kind of influence trading.

Governments and pressure groups

We have noted that the Fifth Republic has often been accused of being unresponsive to the demands of pressure groups. De Gaulle's belief that the French lacked civic sense – by which he meant that they were insufficiently respectful of the State's right to define the national interest – was famous and the social explosion of 1968 was in essence a protest against the arrogant isolationism of his decision-taking style. The political and civil service elites who dominated policy-making in the 1960s and 1970s seemed at times almost equally suspicious of organisations that lacked their commitment to a particular model of economic development. The ease with which France was able to construct a string of nuclear power stations in the 1970s testifies to the absence of official concern with the legitimacy of the consultation process and contrasts with the British experience of lengthy public enquiries.

Yet many commentators have pointed out that the situation is much more complicated than the statist model assumes (Wright 1989, 274ff). French governments cannot, and do not, ignore pressure groups if for no other reason than that their trouble-making can threaten their medium-term survival. Even de Gaulle's government yielded to a miners' strike in 1963 and 1968 was a major victory for its participants, if not for its ideologists. The history of the Fifth Republic is littered with examples of governments giving way to pressure from the streets and from the boardrooms. That this should be so reflects the obvious point that economic Man (and Woman) is also political Man (and Woman). Farmers are vital to the electoral fortunes of the Right in the same way that public sector employees are to the Socialist Party. Thus it is unsurprising that interest groups maintain links with 'friendly' parties, that conservative governments find it very difficult to introduce agricultural reform and socialist ministers pour more and more money into the education system without challenging its organisational bases. The Socialist government of 1981–84 carried out via the Auroux Laws a major package of labour law reform designed, in absolute contrast to the British programme of the same period, to strengthen the institutional rights of trade unionism.

One of the main problems faced by de Gaulle's government during the 1968 crisis was that it needed to negotiate with someone – and if that someone was the Communist-dominated CGT, then this was a price worth paying. The need for recognised negotiators (*interlocuteurs valables*) explains why much public money is spent subsidising organised interests and putting them on official consultative bodies. Workers' and farmers' organisations receive much greater subsidies than their British or American equivalents and it has been calculated that some 4000 public sector employees are on full-time secondment to trade unions (Hall, Hayward, Machin 1990, p. 79). This does not necessarily lead to quiescent behaviour from the recipients;

but hopefully it does provide a semi-institutional basis for negotiation. A reason why recent strikes have been so intractable is that the authority of the 'official' unions has declined at the expense of unofficial 'co-ordinating' committees.

So governments and organised interests share common concerns. To gain support for particular policies, governments need the co-operation of the relevant representative organisations and the latter need the credibility that comes from being recognised as being valid negotiators. Thus the £150 million hastily dished out to farmers in July 1992 in response to new European Community directives enabled the FNSEA to show its members that it was more effective than the militant Confédération Paysanne.

Higher up the decision-taking scale, integration of approved interest groups is widespread and takes two broad forms. On the one hand, there are the close contacts between business and industry and government departments that are facilitated by the traditions of State interventionism and *pantouflage* described in Chapter 4. On the other, there is the attempt to integrate approved groups into decision-taking. The State nominates group representatives to sit on consultative bodies or on the supervisory bodies of France's extensive public and mixed public-private companies. The peak consultative organisation is the (constitutionally recognised) Economic and Social Council, on which cause and sectoral groups are represented. Thousands of other consultative committees exist at national and sub-national level dealing with such issues as social protection, employment, training, energy, housing, the environment etc. Mendras calculates that at least 100,000 activists from different trade unions assume responsibilities in these various spheres (Mendras and Cole 1991, p. 90). The 1988–91 premiership of Michel Rocard was characterised by an attempt to obtain as broad a consensus as possible around legislative proposals, via the organisation of round tables and so on to which concerned pressure groups are invited. One example of this was the attempt to reform the administrative structures of the Ile de France region.

Conclusion

French political discourse makes much use of terms like 'civil society' (*société civile*) and 'the social partners' (*partenaires sociaux*) to describe the organisation of social life. It is difficult not to feel that the benign resonance of such phraseology gives an imperfect picture of the relationships between social categories and between interest groups and government. The French police will carry on hurling tear-gas grenades at demonstrating farmers; the fragmentation and decline of the trade union confederations will continue; French pharmacists will keep on trying to prevent newcomers and supermarkets from muscling in on their lucrative trade. Cosy contacts between business and government elites will flourish, though here the expanding role of the European Community's competition policies is already causing difficulties (see Chapter 10).

What is impressive about French interest groups and their place in the system is the sheer variety of cases. This chapter has shown that interest group fragmentation and governmental hostility in some sectors coexist with influence and integration in others. If the political culture of France remains resistant to the ideology of pluralism, there is no shortage of groups fighting for their cause – or their corner. The success of interest group activity depends, as Vincent Wright shows, on a range of elements, institutional, political and economic. The remorseless decline in the size of France's farming community, like that of Britain's miners, shows that noise alone does not bring results. But the prosperity of many other categories is helped by their access to a State whose very size, as described in Chapter 4, makes it a great provider.

Further reading

James Hollifield and George Ross in Hollifield and Hall (eds), *Searching for the New France*. London: Routledge (1991).

Vincent Wright, *The Government and Politics of France*. London: Unwin Hyman (1989).

France and Europe

The European context of France's politics has always been vital, whether as the 'great power' amongst the ancien régime monarchies or, during the Revolution, as the first ideologically driven modern state. The fact that after 1815 France ceased to be territorially expansionist within Europe did not prevent it from becoming the principal object of Germany's European ambitions and, after 1945, a potential target for the expansion of Soviet communism. Indifference to its European neighbours, let alone splendid isolation or neutralism, has never been an option.

In recent years, commentators have spoken of the Europeanisation of French politics, a concept that can be used in two ways (Hall, Hayward, Machin 1990, p. 1–2). One definition refers to the changes in French political practice and style that are the focus of much of this book – the emergence of executive-led government and of stable electoral coalitions; the secularisation of society and the weakening influence of total belief systems like Catholicism and communism; the decline in the ability, and pretensions, of the State to control economic and social organisation. According to this definition, France is now an example of a common pattern of European politics, rather than a case apart. The second definition of Europeanisation emphasises France's position within the European Community.

France was one of the founder members of the European Economic Community (1957) and its governments have played an influential role in shaping its policy agenda and institutional style. Following the Second World War the Frenchman Jean Monnet mobilised elite support, inside and outside France, for the construction of European institutions, and in the mid-1960s President de Gaulle decisively influenced the way in which Community (EC) institutions would function. Both of his immediate successors influenced the form and content of Community politics, Pompidou by approving Britain's application for entry and Giscard d'Estaing by instituting the European Monetary System and also the regular meetings of EC heads of government known as the European Council. More recently, President Mitterrand and the European Commission president Jacques Delors (who was French finance minister 1981–84) were the central players in the moves towards closer European integration that brought about the Single European Act (1987) and the Maastricht Treaty (1992).

The economic importance of the European Community to France is obvious. In 1992, 63 per cent of its total exports and 60 per cent of its overall imports were with Community countries. But the point about France's Europeanism is that it extends beyond membership of a common market in goods and services. Much official energy is devoted to promoting the idea of France's commitment to a 'European ideal' of economic and political integration that does not exist in other EC members like Britain and Denmark; the French word *communautaire* is used to define a positive attitude towards ever closer European integration. The electoral campaigns of the late 1980s suggested a cross-party consensus about the desirability of European integration, from which only the extra-system parties (PCF and FN) were absent. Opinion polls have regularly shown high levels of public support for Community goals.

What is surprising about this Europeanism is that it exists in a country that before 1957 had a protectionist attitude towards the organisation of international trade; that has, as we have seen, a 'Jacobin' obsession with national sovereignty; and that allows no place in its internal political structures for federalism (see Chapter 6). France is also perceived, from the outside at least, as having an aggressively nationalist foreign policy, symbolised by its independent nuclear deterrent and its refusal to participate in the integrated command structure of the Northern Atlantic Treaty Organisation. Two decades after his death, the long shadow of de Gaulle is still used to explain this perception of France's foreign and defence policies. De Gaulle is identified with two linked propositions, neither of which squares easily with 'European' enthusiasm for political union. One is the belief that the nation state is the only legitimate form of political community and that the greatest crime any state can commit is to hand over sovereignty to another organisation. The other is that a policy of national *grandeur* is the condition of France's very existence as a nation.

Moreover, the result of the 1992 referendum on the ratification of the Maastricht Treaty did not bear out the frequently proclaimed national consensus on European integration. In a high turn-out (70 per cent voted), only 400,000 votes separated the supporters of ratification from its opponents. Referenda are often poor guides to the actual state of public opinion on the issue being decided and act instead as plebiscites on the popularity of the current government. But the size of the 'no' vote on the Maastricht Treaty did suggest that *electoral* opinion was less enthusiastic about closer European integration than earlier *parliamentary* votes had suggested. The market liberalism and political integration implicit in the Single Market Act and the Maastricht Treaty are unwelcome to important sectors of French society (see below).

Such is the complex background to a discussion of France and the European Community. This final chapter seeks to outline the reasons for, and consequences of, France's membership of the European Community and to examine the current state of policy and politics towards it.

Three reasons explain why France takes the Community seriously:

1. Community membership has coincided with, and is often thought to have caused, the great expansion of the French

economy over the last forty years. The Treaty of Rome established both a common market in manufactured goods that incited French industry to break away from its earlier, fearful preference for protected markets and a policy for agriculture that guaranteed the survival of French farming.

2. The Community is a mechanism to bind an economically resurgent Germany to its neighbours and to prevent it from again threatening European, and specifically French, security. For a country that had been invaded by Germany three times in a space of seventy years (1870, 1914, 1940) this was a vital consideration once it became clear in the late-1940s that other powers, and particularly the United States, were not prepared to see Germany remain in the prostrate condition to which its 1945 defeat had reduced it. Fourth Republic governments began the process of political and economic co-operation with West Germany and de Gaulle and his successors have made it the cornerstone of France's European policy. The Community is central to the success of a policy which breaks with the past history of relations between the two countries, yet can only be explained by it.

3. The Community provides a counterweight to the threatened domination by extra-European powers of the medium-sized states of western Europe and acts as a forum for the promotion of France's international interests. For most of the post-war period, the principal threat to the independence of EC states was perceived to come from the Soviet Union and the economic prosperity and co-operation facilitated by the Community helped weaken the domestic appeal of communism. Yet for France, the Community was also a way of preventing the creation of an informal United States hegemony over western Europe. Suspicion of the 'Anglo-Saxons', and their attempts to atlanticise Europe's economy and culture in the name of a spurious internationalism, is never far away from French thinking and rises to the surface at difficult moments like the 1993 crisis in the European Exchange Rate Mechanism. In recent

years a new regional threat has been discerned coming from the industrialised states of south-east Asia. Calls for 'Community preference' are a reminder of France's protectionist past and of the fact that if the European Community is a common market, it is also a customs union, with a common external tariff.

The important point about these three factors is that they are constant. They explain why France joined the Community in the first place and why French governments act as they do in their dealings with other states, notably Germany and the United States. They also show that France's *Europeanism* – like everybody else's – is based on a calculation of *national* interests. There is nothing surprising about this. If European visionaries like Monnet looked forward to the day when national states, and even national communities, would be subsumed in a common European identity, the aim of governments and parties is to protect and to maximise domestic advantage.

What has changed over time are the policy choices deriving from these permanent assumptions about France's interests and the role of the European Community in promoting them.

The Fifth Republic and the European Community: 1958–81

De Gaulle made three durable contributions to France's European policy. In the first place, he reversed his earlier opposition to French membership of the Community and made its free trade ideology the weapon through which French economic modernisation could be realised. In the 1960s French industry moved away from its reliance on protected domestic and colonial markets and successfully penetrated the new 'home market' created by the EEC. At a time when manufacturing exports boomed, the share of the former colonies in France's export markets has declined from 38 per cent in the early 1950s to 5 per cent in the mid-1980s. Simultaneously France ensured that the EEC establish a Common Agricultural Policy that would permit French farming to survive as a major industry. The massive decline in the number of French farmers during the Fifth Republic conceals an increase in agricultural production between 1960 and 1980 of 64 per cent (Flockton and Kofman 1989, p. 145).

De Gaulle' second contribution to the shape of Community development was to sabotage the supra-nationalist aspirations of European idealists like Jean Monnet, Walter Hallstein (the first president of the European Commission) and their supporters in France (notably in the Christian Democratic *Mouvement Républicain Populaire*). For de Gaulle, as we have seen, the only reality was the nation state and the only true Europe was one of nation-states (a *Europe des patries*) in which elected governments made all the important decisions. His opposition to attempts to strengthen the powers of the supra-national bodies of the Community – Parliament and Commission – led to a French boycott of EC institutions and to the 1966 Luxembourg Compromise. This asserted the decision-taking primacy of the Council of Ministers, which brings together the member states, over the Commission and European Parliament.

The third area in which de Gaulle sought to shape the Community was in the construction of a political and diplomatic identity separate from the United States. While accepting French membership of the Atlantic Alliance as a bulwark against the Soviet Union, and giving strong support to President Kennedy in his confrontation with the Soviet leader Khrushchev in the 1962 Cuban missile crisis, de Gaulle tried to challenge United States' influence over the foreign and security, and also economic, policies of its allies. Withdrawal of French troops from the integrated command structure of the North Atlantic Treaty Organisation was one consequence of this and criticism of American foreign (Vietnam) and monetary policies a second. The double veto (1963, 1967) on Britain's entry into the Community reflected de Gaulle's belief that Britain was a 'Trojan horse' for American influence. De Gaulle had little success in shifting other Community members, particularly

West Germany, away from their commitment to American-led Atlanticism towards French-led Europeanism for the simple reason that France's tiny nuclear deterrent (the *bombinette*) was no substitute for Washington's nuclear arsenal. Indeed Gaullist gestures of diplomatic independence actually depended on the continuing United States guarantee to defend western Europe against any Soviet aggression. But even gesture politics can be influential and de Gaulle's actions did highlight the potential for autonomy of the European Community states within an international system dominated by the two superpowers. The 1963 Treaty of Friendship France signed with West Germany became the basis of durable co-operation between the two countries inside the Community.

The institutional legacy of de Gaulle's presidency to the Community was the Luxembourg Compromise. So far as French politics is concerned, his hostility to Community supra-nationalism highlights the differences within the Right between Europeans and nationalists. But it should also be noted that de Gaulle succeeded in reconciling the bulk of the French Right to membership of the Community and in consolidating a lasting consensus around his belief that the interests of the Community may legitimately differ from those of the United States.

De Gaulle's two successors modified aspects of his European policy. Pompidou accepted British membership of the Community and put his name to an (abortive) 1973 plan for European monetary union. Coming from the traditionally more 'European' wing of French Conservatism, President Giscard d'Estaing went further by approving direct elections to the European Parliament, and establishing the European Monetary System. These changes did not however affect the basic principles underlying France's European policy. British membership of the EC was seen as a way of countering the ever-increasing economic power of West Germany and Giscard resisted attempts by the Commission President to increase his institutional authority by being given the right to represent the Community at summits of the Group of Seven industrial nations. He also continued the central plank of Fifth Republic foreign policy – close diplomatic ties with West Germany – and demonstrated a traditional French willingness, after East–West relations deteriorated in 1980, not to treat the Soviet Union as an international pariah.

The Mitterrand Presidency and the European Community

The victory of the Left in 1981 brought to power a Socialist government committed to public ownership and an interventionist industrial policy and sceptical of the virtues of the free market. In 1983, however, President Mitterrand took the decisive step of responding to a major economic crisis provoked by inflation, balance of payments deficits and a depreciating currency by confirming France's commitment to the free trade and monetary disciplines of the Community. This meant a rejection of the alternative 'socialist' strategy advocated by some on the Left, by which France would leave the European Monetary System and erect protectionist controls on Community imports in order to develop its national industrial base. Henceforth, a strong franc, free trade across national borders and company profitability were the proclaimed watchwords of France's economic policy.

The 'European choice' represented by the 1983 measures was confirmed by a series of further Community decisions in which Mitterrand played a central role: the 1984 agreement on Britain's Community payments, the 1985 Single European Act and the 1991 Maastricht Treaty establishing a European Union. The two latter are significant events in France's economic and political evolution. On the one hand they have made it more difficult for the State to intervene in the market, either by the protection of declining industries, or by the use of concealed subsidies to strategically important companies, or by competitive devaluation of the currency. They have also assumed a commitment to the deepening (*approfondissement*) of Community institutions and the acceptance of majority voting in the Council of Ministers. Maastricht in particular represents a challenge to existing concepts of national sovereignty. It deprives individual states of their power to determine monetary policy and their right to have their own currency. It also enables citizens of the Community to exercise political rights (voting in municipal elections) which have hitherto been the prerogative of French citizens.

For all that the integration policies of the late-1980s marked a significant advance on what had gone before, France's 'European choice' does not constitute a break with the three principles described at the beginning of the chapter. Instead it emphasises the role of the European Community as the forum in which French national interests can best be defended:

1. The concern that the Community countries should not be dominated by the economic, technological and diplomatic clout of extra-European powers remains. Mitterrand originated the European technology programme EUREKA as a means of countering American advances in the field. More recently French intransigence on the GATT agreements on liberalising world trade showed the continued existence of elite – and popular – resentment at American economic power. To this fear of the United States should be added the already noted fear of Japanese influence in European markets which is absent in other Community members, notably Britain.

2. Like de Gaulle and Pompidou before him, President Mitterrand has established a special relationship with the head of Germany's government (Chancellor Kohl). Inter-governmental co-operation is highly institutionalised. Yet concern about German power continues to haunt French policy makers. The collapse of the Soviet Empire in 1989–91 and the failure of French diplomatic moves to slow down the subsequent rush to German reunification suggested that the shared decision-taking processes of the European Community were the only way for France to exercise control over its ever more powerful neighbour.

Community deepening (*approfondissement*) – be it monetary (a common currency), diplomatic (a common foreign and security policy), military (the creation in 1992 of a 3,500-strong Franco-German military corps) or institutional (greater use of majority voting in the Council of Ministers) – is France's way of binding Europe's giant to its neighbours. As Stephen George writes: 'In order to reassert some control over its own monetary and economic affairs it became Mitterrand's policy to press for closer integration, so as to move away from a situation in which the French economy was regulated primarily by decisions made in the Federal Republic' (George 1991, p. 92). For all the reality of present day Franco-German co-operation, memories of past disasters still surface when the issue of Europe's future is being debated. In the 1992 referendum both advocates and opponents of Maastricht constantly referred to the potential threat from across the Rhine. The role of the Bundesbank in destabilising the Exchange Rate Mechanism (ERM) in Summer 1993 led to great resentment.

3. President Mitterrand has laid great emphasis on the social dimension of Europe, by which he means extending employees' rights and social benefits. This derives from the fear of 'social dumping' (multi-national companies going to countries where labour is cheap) and of the competitive advantage gained by countries that refuse such rights as well as from socialism. It also speaks to a wider political consensus within France about the virtues of collective welfare provision that extends to the Christian Democrat tradition with the UDF and the populist traditions of Gaullism. In the same way, the Maastricht Treaty provisions for European industrial and regional policies reflect enduring French beliefs in the effectiveness of governmental interventionism in promoting balanced economic development.

4. The Common Agricultural Policy is still a vital policy area given the electoral importance of the farming vote and the

fact that France is the world's second largest exporter of agricultural products.

5. France has not seriously tried to change the decision-taking structures of the Community by promoting the power of its supra-national institutions, notably the European Parliament. Enthusiasts for European integration were disappointed at the very limited increase in the powers of the Parliament conceded by the Maastricht Treaty. France did not make this a central issue.

Domestic policy and politics

Policy

European integration affects the capacity of parliaments and governments to determine policy. At its most basic, the primacy of Community over national law has been confirmed by France's highest administrative court, the Council of State, which in October 1990 acknowledged that the French parliament could not legislate in contradiction with Community regulations and directives. Some of France's local authorities have responded enthusiastically to the regionalist dimension that springs from Community integration policy by grouping together to open offices in Brussels.

Even under de Gaulle the Common Agricultural Policy meant that farming policy would henceforth be determined by decisions taken jointly in Brussels rather than in Paris. In recent years, the competition policies of the Single European Act have restricted the ability of France's extensive public sector companies to make investment decisions. Community free trade agreements have provoked anger from prominent industrialists, like the boss of the Peugeot car firm, who accuses Brussels of opening the European market to unfair competition from Japanese manufacturers. The high interest rates necessary to protect the franc within the Exchange Rate Mechanism helped push France into recession in 1992. Another problem arises from the harmonisation of the tax systems of the member states of the Community. France relies much more heavily than its neighbours on indirect taxation, notably VAT, and on social insurance contributions for its tax base (only 20 per cent of fiscal resources derive from income tax). It has been estimated that Community proposals to introduce two harmonised VAT bands would deprive the French Exchequer of 40 billion francs and that companies' social insurance payments will have to fall if industry is to remain competitive in a single market. France is also now a net contributor to the EC budget.

Politics

In recent years the bulk of France's mainstream political forces have allied themselves with the cause of closer integration in the European Community. One sign of this was the ease with which the National Assembly in 1991 approved the Schengen Agreement whereby France and four (later seven) other Community members agreed to trust each other's border controls and permit free flows of peoples across each other's frontiers. Only 61 deputies voted against the agreement compared with 495 in favour. In June 1992 the Congress of deputies and senators comfortably voted both the constitutional amendments required for Maastricht to be ratified and then the Treaty itself.

European integrationism has caused little anguish to some of France's political families. The Christian Democratic origins of the Centre des Démocrates Sociaux (CDS) means that it has always been dedicated to the ideal of European unity and, with relatively few exceptions, the Republican Party backs the commitment to the values of Maastricht of its founder Giscard d'Estaing. The Parti Socialiste too has a long history, stretching back to the Fourth Republic, of attachment to the cause of European integration. Since the mid-1980s, Mitterrand has sought to make Europe the core of the new definition of Socialism. The nationalist and statist group within the party, led by Jean Pierre Chevènement, criticises the free market philosophy of the Community and the multinationals' Europe established by Maastricht. But it is much weaker than it was and Chevènement has now (1993) left the party. Despite the Socialist Party's 1993 defeat, its leadership has maintained the official pro-Europeanism.

By contrast, the Communists and Front National (and sections of the ecology movement) use France's European policy as part of their general hostility to the system. The PCF has always been hostile to the European Community, which it regards as an agent of international, and particularly American/German, capital. It has denounced Commission plans for the rationalisation of traditional industries like steel, and at its most recent conference all but advocated French withdrawal from the Community. In June 1992 its parliamentary group was the only one to vote *en bloc* against the constitutional amendment necessary for the ratification of Maastricht, and in the subsequent referendum it used the threat to the guarantees of public sector workers posed by the treaty. The Front National is not, of course, hostile to private ownership and it loudly proclaims the need to defend European culture. But its vision of Europe, like its vision of France, is culturally restrictive and racist and the defence it promises takes the form of attacks on the 'threat' of cultural and racial degeneration posed by Islam and by multinational, rootless finance capital. As the defender of the 'ordinary Frenchman' against big government and high taxation, the Front National denounces Brussels interventionism; the 'France first' rhetoric used against immigrants is also employed against the 'federasts' who would destroy national identity.

The position of the neo-Gaullist RPR is more complex. De Gaulle's vision of a *Europe des patries* had no room for supra-nationalism and the values, if not always the practice, of Gaullism tended to favour the sort of dirigist interventionism that fits uneasily into Community competition policy. In 1979, the RPR leader Chirac ran a stridently nationalist and anti-integrationist campaign in the European elections. Over the last ten years leadership attitudes have evolved (see Chapter 9). The neo-liberal economic policies espoused by the RPR leadership led to a greater enthusiasm for the completed single market and to the toning down of opposition to political integration. In the 1988 presidential election the Gaullist candidate Chirac did not attack the provisions of the Single Market Act and four years later he supported the ratification of the Maastricht Treaty, knowing that not to do so would ruin his future hopes of the presidency. The RPR prime minister since 1993, Balladur, is committed to the Single Market and to Maastricht.

Maastricht, however, has revealed the existence of doubts within the RPR about the desirability of the 1980s moves to European integration. In 1992 a sizeable segment of the parliamentary party, and even more of the activists, rallied to the anti-federalist, pro-sovereignty campaign led by Philippe Seguin and Charles Pasqua with the support of influential elder statesmen like ex-prime ministers Debré and Messmer and de Gaulle's long-serving foreign minister Couve de Murville. Pierre Lefranc, president of the *Association de fidélité au General de Gaulle*, was a founder member of the anti-Maastricht *Comité pour une autre Europe*. Seguin and Pasqua organised an effective anti-Maastricht campaign in Summer 1992. After the 1993 elections, Seguin returned to the attack on the dangers of political and economic union and employed two significant historical analogies to do so. Maastricht was portrayed as the betrayal of the principles of national sovereignty and citizen unity proclaimed by the 1789 Revolution – and as a 'social Munich' that deprived government of its power to mobilise national energies against unemployment.

It is tempting to identify the RPR divisions over European integration with those in the British Conservative Party. There are however significant differences. The anti-Maastricht Conservatives' commitment to unrestricted free markets and to rolling back the collective provision of welfare has less meaning to RPR critics of the Treaty, who have a Gaullist belief in the virtues of statist solutions to economic and social problems. Indeed, the opposition of some neo-Gaullists to the Maastricht Treaty helped the RPR in 1993 to regain some of the popular vote which it had earlier lost; it won 22 per cent of workers' votes and 22 per cent of unemployed. The comparable figures for the strongly pro-Maastricht UDF are 10 per cent and 8 per cent.

Conclusion: Maastricht and France's European choice

The closeness of the 1992 referendum result conceals significant variations in the pattern of votes. If some of these reflect enduring traditions – the 'yes' vote was strong in Catholic Brittany and Alsace – others indicate the socio-economic geography that Europe has helped to create. A majority voted against ratification in economically depressed departments (Pas de Calais, Dordogne, Allier, Somme) where Mitterrand gained his best results in 1988; by contrast one of the strongest 'yes' votes came in the affluent Hauts de Seine department whose political boss is the anti-Maastricht RPR leader, Charles Pasqua. The 'yes' vote was strongest in cities and amongst the educated middle classes. The 'no' vote obtained its highest scores in areas of industrial decline, in southern towns where the Front National is strong and, above all, in farming regions. Sixty-three per cent of farmers and 61 per cent of workers voted no compared with only 20 per cent of senior, and 39 per cent of middle, managers.

It is unsurprising that at a time of high unemployment, high interest rates and no (rather than low) growth the shine has gone off the 'European choice', too easily advocated by political elites in the 1980s as the painless way in which France could assure its future. The decision to shelve the implementation of the Schengen Agreement abolishing cross-border controls, and the Balladur government's intransigent attitudes towards agreed Community positions on the GATT talks, are evidence of this reflection of the darker climate of the 1990s. Both the RPR and, to a lesser extent, the PS contain elements who may yet be tempted to raise the national drawbridge against continuing integration. The 1993 crisis within the European Monetary System was particularly serious in that it presented a threat to each of the three components of France's European option. Economically, it challenged the central plank of French economic policy – the strong franc tied to the mark; diplomatically, it reminded everyone of the power of Germany's central bank to determine 'European' outcomes; politically, it threatened the credibility of the governing parties, on both Right and Left, who had fashioned the European policy and made it one of the elements of the new consensus.

A breakdown in this consensus – and in the Franco-German axis that is its core – would embarrass many members of France's political and economic elites. This fact alone may help to explain why the system parties closed ranks around the Mitterrand/Balladur axis in the ERM crisis and why French irritation with German decisions has not produced a breakdown in bilateral relations. But there is more to the continuing solidity of the European choice than embarrassment. The Maastricht referendum and sectoral discontent notwithstanding, little evidence exists to suggest that the disillusion of ordinary voters with those who in the 1980s consolidated France's European choice extends to the policy itself. Like the Fifth Republic, 'Europe' is now part of France's institutional and political landscape. Landscapes are, of course, vulnerable to earthquakes; but so far the fault lines in France's institutional and European order have been contained.

Further reading

S. George, *Policy and Politics in the European Community*. Oxford University Press (1991).

Appendix

Facts and figures

1. The construction of France

The origins of what is called France are generally dated from the division of the Carolingian Empire agreed in 843 by the Treaty of Verdun and from the election as king of Hugh Capet in 987. Although other rulers, and notably the kings of England, once owned large parts of present-day France, the French Monarchy managed over the centuries to extend its authority from its base in the Ile de France into the southern regions of Occitania (where French was not spoken), into independent principalities like Burgundy and Brittany and into Alsace and Franche Comté. The eastern region of Lorraine did not become part of France until 1776, twelve years after the Mediterranean island of Corsica, which is 200 kilometers from the nearest French coastline, was acquired. Thus the frontiers of present-day France were more or less established by the French Revolution, with Nice and Savoy being attached in 1860.

The doctrine of France's 'natural frontiers' dates from the seventeenth century. In modern times, the principal challenge to France's territorial integrity has come from Germany, which annexed the frontier regions of Alsace and Lorraine between 1871–1918 and 1940–44. One peculiarity of the juridical definition of France is that it includes territories located thousands of miles away from the mainland (which is known, because of its shape, as the hexagon). 'France' exists in the Indian Ocean, the West Indies, the North Atlantic and the South Pacific as well as in Europe.

2. The French nation

Area	549,000 sq. km
Population	56.3 million (mainland), 1.4 million overseas territories, 1.5 million abroad
Immigrant population	3.7 million
Population density	102 sq km
Urban population	82%
GDP 1991	3,023 billion francs

% Distribution of the working population by sector and period:

	1870	1913	1950	1973	1990
Agriculture	49.2	37.4	28.5	11.0	5.7
Industry	27.8	33.8	34.8	38.4	28.1
Services	23.0	28.0	36.7	50.6	66.2

3. French regimes since 1789

1789–92	Constitutional Monarchy
1792–99	First Republic
1799–1814	Consulate of Napoleon and first Empire
1814–30	Bourbon Monarchy
1830–48	July Monarchy (Louis Philippe)
1848–52	Second Republic
1852–70	Second Empire (Napoleon III)
1870–1940	Third Republic
1940–44	French State (Marshal Pétain)
1944–46	Provisional Government
1946–58	Fourth Republic
1958–	Fifth Republic

4. Electoral systems in the Fifth Republic

Election	System	Electoral constituency
Presidency	two ballot, first-past-the-post	whole country
National Assembly	two ballots, first-past-the-post	single-member constituency
European Parliament	proportional by list	whole country
Senate	indirect, electoral college	department
Regional Council	proportional by list	department
Departmental Council	two ballot, first-past-the-post	canton
Municipal Council		
(a) under 3500 pop.	two ballot, winner-takes-all	commune
(b) over 3500 pop.	two ballot, 50% winner: 50% proportionally	commune (except Paris, Lyons Marseilles)

5. Election results since 1958

National Assembly seats won by the major parties 1958–93

	1958	1962	1967	1968	1973	1978	1981	1986	1988	1993
PCF	10	41	73	34	73	86	44	35	27	24
PS and allies	88	106	121	57	102	115	283	216	275	67
Centre/Right	182	91	85	94	119	123	61	131	131	207
Gaullists	207	233	200	293	183	154	83	155	130	242
FN	–	–	–	–	–	–	–	35	1	–

Second-round presidential election results 1965–1988

	million votes	%	
1965			
de Gaulle	12.6	54.5	elected
Mitterrand	10.6	45.5	
1969			
Pompidou	10.7	57.6	elected
Poher	7.9	42.4	
1974			
Giscard d'Estaing	13.1	50.7	elected
Mitterrand	12.7	49.3	
1981			
Mitterrand	15.7	51.8	elected
Giscard d'Estaing	14.6	48.2	
1988			
Mitterrand	16.7	54.0	elected
Chirac	14.2	46.0	

6. French Prime Ministers 1959–93

M. Debré (Gaullist) 1959–62
G. Pompidou (Gaullist) 1962–68
M. Couve de Murville (Gaullist) 1968–69
J. Chaban-Delmas (Gaullist) 1969–72
P. Messmer (Gaullist) 1972–74
J. Chirac (Gaullist) 1974–76
R. Barre (UDF) 1976–81
P. Mauroy (PS) 1981–84
L. Fabius (PS) 1984–86
J. Chirac (RPR) 1986–88
M. Rocard (PS) 1988–91
E. Cresson (PS) 1991–92
P. Bérégevoy (PS) 1992–93
E. Balladur (RPR) 1993–

Bibliography

The following English language books are particularly useful to students.

A. Cole (ed.) *French Political Parties in Transition*. Aldershot: Dartmouth (1990).

C. Flockton and E. Kofman, *France*. London: Paul Chapman (1989).

J. Frears, *Parties and Voters in France*. London: Hurst (1991).

P. Hall, J. Hayward, H. Machin, *Developments in French Politics*. London: Macmillan (1990).

J. Hayward (ed.) *De Gaulle to Mitterrand*. London: Hurst (1993).

J. Hollifield, P. Hall (eds), *Searching for the New France*. London: Routledge (1991).

J. McMillan, *Twentieth Century France*. London: Edward Arnold (1992).

H. Mendras and A. Cole, *Social Change in Modern France*. Cambridge University Press (1991).

A. Stevens *The Government and Politics of France*. London: Macmillan (1992).

K. Wadia and S. Williams (eds), *France and Europe*. Wolverhampton: ASMCF Books (1993).

V. Wright, *The Government and Politics of France*. London: Unwin Hyman (1989).

The following French language texts are recommended.

O. Duhamel, *Le Pouvoir Politique en France*. Paris: Presses Universitaires de France (1991).

Y. Mény, *Le Système Politique Français*. Paris: Montchrestien (1991).
Y. Mény, *La Corruption de la République*. Paris: Fayard (1992).
P. Rosanvallon, *L'Etat en France*. Paris: Seuil (1990).

A most useful survey of all aspects of contemporary French life is contained in the regularly updated *L'Etat de la France* published in Paris by Editions La Découverte. See especially the 1992 and 1993–94 editions. The quarterly journal, *Modern and Contemporary France*, also contains much useful information and analysis.

Index